THE GOSPEL

FOR KIDS

Series A
ELDON WEISHEIT

Publishing House
St. Louis

The Scripture quotations in this publication are from the Today's English Version of the New Testament. Copyright © American Bible Society 1966, 1971. Third edition, 1973. Used by permission.

Concordia Publishing House, St. Louis, Missouri
MANUFACTURED IN THE UNITED STATES OF AMERICA
3 4 5 6 7 8 9 10 11 12 1B 90 89 88 87 86 85 84 83 82 81

Library of Congress Cataloging in Publication Data

Weisheit, Eldon
        The Gospel for kids, series A.

        1. Children's sermons.   I. Title.
BV4315.W373   252′.53   77-9601
ISBN 0-570-03265-2

Preface

If you read this book in one sitting, you will find it repetitious. The same message shows up on every other page. Jesus Christ is your Savior. By His life, death, and life, He has changed your life and death because He has given you eternal life.

But the book is not to be read. It is to be shared. The book assumes that its message is being sprinkled into lives that include fear, temptation, guilt, disappointment, boredom as well as fun, excitement, joy, and peace.

Because Christ came to live with us, His action applies to every part of our lives. When we cry, Jesus is there to cry with us. When we laugh, He joins in.

The Gospel of Christ is never dull or repetitious to those who apply it to all areas of their own lives. To preach the Gospel to kids, or to anyone else, you must first feel the joy and comfort of Christ in your own life. You must know that you need it. And you must know that it works.

If you are to preach the Gospel to kids, or to anyone else, you must not only talk to them but also listen to them. Know the joys and problems of the people with whom you share the Gospel. Listen to their reactions—not just their reactions to your sermons but their reactions to life situations. Then tell them that Jesus shares that situation.

Maybe the object lessons in this book will help apply Christ to the situations in your life. I hope so. If they do, they will also help you apply Christ to the situations in the lives of the kids in your care.

Eldon Weisheit

Scripture Index

The homilies in this book are based on portions of the Gospels selected by the Inter-Lutheran Commission on Worship, Year A.

To my son Wes
on his fifteenth birthday
for adding to the challenge and reward of preaching

Contents

Be Ready for the Good News

The Word

For this reason, then, you also must be always ready, because the Son of Man will come at an hour when you are not expecting Him. Matthew 24:44 (From the Gospel for the First Sunday in Advent)

The World

A shoeshine kit, two pairs of scuffed shoes, a pair of polished shoes.

When you see this (shoeshine kit) waiting on your chair, you know what your job is. You must polish shoes for your father. And that's a job (show scuffed shoes). But this pair (polished) looks good. If you polish them a little with a cloth, they'll be ready to wear. So you can watch TV after all.

When your father asks for a pair of shoes, you give him these (polished). But he says, "I want to wear these" (scuffed). So you weren't ready after all. Even though you had one pair polished, you did not have the pair that your father needed ready for him.

Our Bible reading tells us to be ready for Christ's coming. He will come to judge us; that is, to look at our lives. He wants to see if we have received the gifts of love and forgiveness that He brought to us when He came to be our Savior long ago. He wants to know if we are ready to go to heaven with Him.

We can have parts of our lives ready, just as one pair of shoes was ready. We are here now; so we could tell Him, "See, Lord, we like to hear Your Word and worship You." We could also say that we love some people, that we forgive some people, and that we help some people.

But that kind of preparation is like having only one pair of shoes polished. When Jesus comes, He is not coming to look at

9

only parts of our lives. He wants us to be prepared for Him in all that we do.

The Bible reading says we do not know when He is coming. His purpose in not telling us when He will come is not so He can sneak up on us. It is not because He wants to find us doing something wrong.

Instead, Jesus wants us to know that we need the Good News of His love in all parts of our lives. He does not want us to prepare only a part of our lives, but He wants us to use that Good News every moment that we live. And when we have His love with us at all times, we are prepared for His coming.

Think about areas of your life which are already prepared. You know Jesus loves you. You share that love with some people. You help some people because Jesus gives you the power to love them. Those parts of your life are like the one pair of polished shoes. You are ready for Christ because Christ is already with you.

But also look at other parts of your life. See areas where you are tempted or where you do wrong. See places where you know or think you might not be ready for Jesus. Then know that Christ comes also to those parts of your life. He comes to bring Good News to you every moment that you are alive—and He promises that you will live forever.

Make a Straight Path

The Word

"Turn away from your sins," he [John the Baptist] said "because the kingdom of heaven is near!" John was the one that the prophet Isaiah was talking about when he said, "Someone is shouting in the desert, 'Get the Lord's road ready for Him; make a straight path for Him to travel!'" Matthew 3:2-3 (From the Gospel for the Second Sunday in Advent)

The World

A maze on a large poster (or a transparency for an overhead projector) which has an entry and a destination, called home; however, the paths are blocked so one cannot travel from the entry to the destination. A long narrow strip (or a second transparency) with a straight road with several places to enter on either side. The strip should be long enough to reach from "home" to any part of the maze.

When John the Baptist told people to turn away from their sins because the kingdom of heaven was near, he might have pictured them in a maze like this. The place called home is the kingdom of heaven. We are all in the paths around it in the maze. We have to make decisions to go this way or that way. We sometimes come to a dead end and have to decide: do we turn around and try again or do we just stay at the dead end and pretend it is where we belong.

Can you imagine yourself in this kind of a maze? You wonder whether you should go this way or that. You face a temptation, a decision, an opportunity. Even when you know the way you should go, you often turn the other direction. You walk with other people in your family, class, or church. Some pull you one way and some say to go the other way.

When we look at a maze like this, we can see ahead and avoid the dead ends and wrong turns. But in life we have to live

11

day by day. We have to take the chance on being wrong. And John's advice, "Turn away from sin," doesn't help that much, because we manage to find sin any direction we go.

But John also gave another message. He was the one that an Old Testament prophet had said would come to announce: "Get the Lord's road ready for Him; make a straight path for Him to travel." John told the people to get ready for Christ.

And we are getting ready for Christ as we prepare to celebrate Christmas. We need to get a road ready for Him. A straight path for Him to travel. (Add the straight road.) This makes the maze easier to travel. This straight path can swing around to connect any part of the maze with home. It has places for people to enter at any point. If you were caught at a dead end like this, the road comes to you and gives you a way out. No longer do you have to wonder which way to go. You see the straight path home.

Christ is the way of eternal life. He rescues us from all the problems of this life and takes us home. But He does even more than that. Notice that the text does not say, "Make a straight path so we can travel to Him." It says, "Make a straight path for Him to travel." He makes the first trip. He comes to us. He comes to each part of our lives to help us. He gives us His strength when we are tempted. He comes to forgive us when we are wrong. He guides us when we are lost.

We prepare for His coming by seeing a straight path from God to all parts of our own lives and also to the lives of other people.

Look for a Real Christmas

The Word

Jesus said, "How happy is he who has no doubts about Me!" Matthew 11:6
(From the Gospel for the Third Sunday in Advent)

The World

A branch from an artificial Christmas tree and another from a real evergreen.

These two branches may look the same from a distance, and in some ways they are alike. But there is also a great difference between them. This is from a real Christmas tree. And this is from an artificial tree. You can see, feel, and smell the differences when you are near the two branches.

It's easy to tell the difference between a real and artificial Christmas tree, but can you tell the difference between a real and an artificial Christmas?

Maybe you never thought about it, but you can have an artificial Christmas. Just as the artificial tree can serve a purpose, an artificial Christmas can be fun. You can give and receive presents, go to parties, sing songs and still not have a real Christmas.

A real Christmas includes the coming of God's Son to be a part of life with people on earth. On the first Christmas He came as the Baby at Bethlehem. But the Baby was God, and He came to be the Savior. Now He continues to come as the Savior who gives new life to people who know and believe this.

When Jesus was here the first time, some people wanted to know for sure that He was the real Savior. They did not want an artificial Son of God. Jesus told them to look at what He did. He healed the blind, deaf, and crippled. He brought a dead person back to life. He had a message of love and hope for all people. They could tell that He was real because what He did was real. His action proved that His words were true.

Just as Jesus pointed to what He did for people to show that He was a real and not an artificial Savior, you can tell if your Christmas is real by seeing what it does for you. Ask yourself some questions:

Will this Christmas help me feel the presence of God? Will I realize that He not only came to a manger but also to me? Will I see again how much God loves me and feel that love in action? Will I see that He came not only for me but for all people? And will I love others because He loves me?

Prepare now to celebrate a real Christmas. Recognize that many things that look like Christmas offer only an artificial Christmas. They are not wrong, but don't use them as a substitute for the real thing.

Christmas is real when you know Christ comes to you. Then you will have a merry Christmas, because the promise Jesus made in our Bible reading will come true. He said, "How happy is he who has no doubts about Me!" You need have no doubt that Jesus loves you, that He is your Savior, and that He will always be with you. That's a real Christmas!

Get the Connection

The Word

While he was thinking about this, an angel of the Lord appeared to him in a dream and said, "Joseph, descendant of David, do not be afraid to take Mary to be your wife. For it is by the Holy Spirit that she has conceived. She will give birth to a Son and you will name Him Jesus—because He will save His people from their sins." Matthew 1:20-21 (From the Gospel for the Fourth Sunday in Advent)

The World

An electric light plugged into a source of electricity, a string of electric tree lights, an adapter.

Before Jesus was born, Joseph, Mary's husband-to-be, noticed she was expecting a baby. He knew he wasn't the baby's father. He was worried. But God spoke to him in a dream. We hear what God said in the Bible reading for today, "Joseph, descendant of David, do not be afraid to take Mary to be your wife. For it is by the Holy Spirit that she has conceived. She will give birth to a Son and you will name Him Jesus—because He will save His people from their sins."

Joseph knew God had promised to send a Savior to the world. He knew that people needed the Savior. But like other people at that time, Joseph had not known how God was going to give help to people.

Maybe this illustration will help us understand God's way of helping us. We want to light these Christmas tree lights. But they need electricity. Here is a light. It has electricity. See—it works. (Turn the light on.) This light has electricity. These lights need electricity. But we have no way to get the power from the one to the other.

No way, that is, unless we have one of these. (Show

adapter.) This adapter can be a part of the tree lights. See how the plug on the lights fits into the adapter. (Put the plug in the adapter. Remove it.) This adapter also fits the light. (Remove the bulb from the light and screw the adapter in.) Because the adapter fits both the light socket and the tree light, it can be used as a connection for the two. See, we can put them all together, and the electricity from the socket lights up the tree lights.

We are like the tree lights. We need a source of power. God is like the big light. He is the source of power. Jesus is the adapter. Because He is God, He fits in the socket with the electricity. Because He was born of a human mother, He fits into our lives. He is the source of power that we can plug into for help.

God told Joseph that Jesus was conceived by the Holy Spirit. This was important—so everyone would know that He is God. It was also important that Jesus was born of a human mother—so we would know that He is a person and a part of our lives. As we prepare for Christmas, we need to know that Jesus is both God and man. He is God so we can receive God's power and love for us. He is a person so He can deliver that power to us.

Get the connection.

Look for the Right Clue

The Word

The angel said to them [the shepherds], "Don't be afraid! I am here with good news for you, which will bring great joy to all the people. This very day in David's town your Savior was born—Christ, the Lord! What will prove it to you is this: you will find a Baby wrapped in cloths and lying in a manger." Luke 2:10-12 (From the Christmas Gospel)

The World

A toy or a child's game wrapped as a Christmas gift.

Christmas has many mysteries. When we wrap a gift, we make a mystery because no one knows what is in it. This present has several mysteries. You don't know what is in it. But you don't know who it is for or who it is from either because there is no tag on it. So you'll have to watch for clues to solve the mystery.

Let me give you one clue that will solve all the mysteries about this package. It is a (name the gift). Now we'll have to see if my clue is right. (Open the gift.) It is. Now you know what is in the package and you also know who it is from. I knew what was in the package even before it was opened. That means the gift was from me. I gave you the clue, which shows I knew what was in the package.

The angel who told the shepherds about the birth of Jesus also gave them a clue. The angel said, "This very day in David's town your Savior was born—Christ the Lord! What will prove it to you is this: you will find a Baby wrapped in cloths and lying in a manger."

When the shepherds found the Baby exactly as the angel had said, they knew that the Baby was a special gift from God because God's angel had given them the clue that was true.

The angel also gave a clue to us. He said, "I am here with good news for you, which will bring great joy to all the people." The clue is that all people will have great joy. That joy will come from the good news that God kept His promises and sent His Son to earth to be the Savior for all people.

Now we have to look for the clue in our lives. Are you filled with great joy? Are you happy because you know God loves you? Are you happy because you know the Baby born in Bethlehem lived for you and gave His life in your place so you could live forever with Him? Are you happy because you know Jesus is with you today?

If you are happy today because Jesus is your Savior, you have a clue from God. God's angel promised joy to all people who heard the good news about the Savior. God knew that His gift to us was a good gift. He knew that Jesus could and would do what had to be done to save all people from their sin.

When you feel joy today because Christ is your Savior, you have a clue from God. You know the gift you have came from Him.

Christmas on the Run

The Word

After they [the Wise Men] had left, an angel of the Lord appeared in a dream to Joseph and said, "Get up, take the Child and His mother and run away to Egypt, and stay there until I tell you to leave. Herod will be looking for the Child to kill Him." Matthew 2:13 (From the Gospel for the First Sunday After Christmas)

The World

If the church or classroom still has a variety of Christmas decorations including a creche, use as is. If not, collect a variety of Christmas items including a creche.

Look at all the Christmas decorations we have. Think how our church will look in a few days when the decorations are all put away. Each year we bring out all the lights, the manger scene, the candles, and we get a tree. These decorations remind us that God kept His promises and sent His Son to live with us.

But what if we don't have time to put all the decorations away this year? If we had only a minute to take what we wanted, what would we choose? The most important decoration is the Baby in the manger. Others may cost more, but all of them point to Him. If we could have only one thing to keep for next year, it would be the Baby.

Joseph and Mary had to make such a choice. After Jesus was born, they moved into a house in Bethlehem. They planned to stay in the town where they had relatives. They were the center of attention there. The shepherds had told everyone about the song of the angels. All their neighbors knew they had had important visitors from a faraway land who gave them expensive gifts. Everyone in the little town must have come to see them.

Then an angel told them they had to leave town immediately. They had to go to a strange country where no one knew about the angels or the Wise Men. They would be just a young married couple with a baby.

But they had the Baby. And the Baby was God's Son. They could leave everthing else behind because they had the one gift that had been promised to them.

When you leave Christmas behind and start a new year, make sure you take the Baby with you. All the other things of Christmas were nice. It was fun to have parties and get presents. The decorations were beautiful. But Jesus is the gift from God.

The other things of Christmas will break, wear out, be forgotten, or get lost. But Jesus will be with you at all times. Think of Joseph and Mary as they had to run for their lives. They carried the Baby with them. They were safe. You may face problems in the new year. But keep God's gift with you and you will always have His help. Take not just the doll baby from the creche but the Savior in your heart.

Check Your Road Map

The Word

A week later, when the time came for the Baby to be circumcised, He was named Jesus, the name which the angel had given Him before He had been conceived. Luke 2:21 (From the Gospel for The Name of Jesus)

The World

A large road map with an *X* at the place where the sermon is preached and another *X* at a city across the map. Also draw a circle around several places on the route between the two *X*s.

One week ago we celebrated the birth of Jesus. God sent His Son to be our Savior. In some ways the life of Jesus is like a trip. If you planned a trip, you would use a road map like this. We are here. We plan to go there. If we travel from here to here, we will go through many places along the way. Some of them are marked with circles. If, as we travel, we discover we are here (a place off the route) instead of here (circled place), we would know we have taken a wrong road. We'd have to get back on the right road.

We see the life of Jesus as a trip if we think of Him as being born here (the first *X*). He came to earth to die for our sins and to rise from the grave. That's His destination over here. God also planned things for Jesus to do between His birth and resurrection. We see two of them in today's Bible reading. Jesus was circumcised one week after He was born. Like all boys, He was marked to show he belonged to God's chosen people. And His parents named Him Jesus as the angel had told them to do.

Both the circumcusion and the name of Jesus show that His life was on course. Those events are like circles on our map. He was going the right way. He was keeping the Law for us even when He was eight days old.

21

Our lives are also planned. We are born here (first *X*), and when we die, we go to heaven here (second *X*). But we do not wait until the time we die to see if we are on the right road. Jesus has given us many places in our lives to see if we are going the way He has told us to go.

He told us to be baptized. When you remember your baptism and know that God has given you a new life, you are checking to see if you are on course. He has told you to be sorry for your sins when you have done wrong and He will forgive you. When you repent and receive forgiveness, you are checking the map to see if you are on course and correcting any mistakes. He has told us to love other people, to help those in need, to study His Word, to worship Him. When we do those things in His name, we are on the road He has given us.

On this first day of a new year each of us should check our lives to see if we are on course. Are you following the road that Jesus gave you? Are you heading toward the eternal life He has promised? If so, thank God that He is guiding your life. If you feel you are off course, now is the time to look at the map and get back on the right road.

An Invitation You Can Accept

The Word

God gave the Law through Moses; but grace and truth came through Jesus Christ. John 1:17 (From the Gospel for the Second Sunday After Christmas)

The World

Two sealed envelopes, each with a note (see below) and one with an airline ticket or check.

Here are two letters. Let's pretend the letters are addressed to you. Each of them is from a friend who lives in (name a city several hundreds miles away). So let's read the mail.

The first note says: "Hi! I'd like for you to spend next weekend with me. Why don't you fly out here? I'll meet you at the airport and we'll have a great time. Let me know if you can come." And it's signed by your friend.

That sounds like fun. But what if you don't have the money to buy the airplane ticket. Then you'd have to say, "I'm sorry, I can't visit you now."

But we have another letter to open. It says: "Hi! I'd like for you to spend next weekend with me. Why don't you fly out here. I'll meet you at the airport and we'll have a great time. Here is your airplane ticket [or check]." And it is signed by your friend.

Both letters give you the same invitation. Both want you to do the same thing. But there is a great difference between the two. The second letter not only asks you to do something but it also gives you the way to do it.

Our Bible reading tells us about two messages from God. It says, first of all, "God gave the Law through Moses." You know the Law. It tells you what you must do to lead a good life. It also tells you what you must not do. The Law is a gift from

23

God. If we follow the Law we will be much happier than if we disobey the Law.

The Law is like the first letter. It asks us to do something that we cannot do. We cannot be perfect and do everything that God has asked us to do.

But God has also sent us another message. The Bible reading says, "But grace and truth came through Jesus Christ." When Jesus came to earth, He did not just tell us what to do and what not to do. He did the good things for us and let us share in His goodness. He made up for the bad things that we have done by giving Himself to pay for our sin.

Jesus is like the second letter from the friend. He gives us the way to make the trip to God. His gift of grace is a ticket that lets us come to God. He is the truth that tells us God loves us and wants to be with us always.

Look on Both Sides

The Word

Soon afterwards some men who studied the stars came from the east to Jerusalem and asked: "Where is the Baby born to be the king of the Jews? We saw His star when it came up in the east, and we have come to worship Him." When King Herod heard about this, he was very upset, and so was everyone else in Jerusalem. Matthew 2:1b-3 (From the Gospel for Epiphany)

The World

Two posters with a door drawn on both sides of each. On the bars of one poster write "Push" on one side and "Pull" on the other. On the other, the words "Repent" and "Believe."

If you were walking into a building and saw this door (show the one that says "pull") you would know what to do. You would pull the door open (do it) and walk through. If you were to leave the building by the same door you might remember that it said to pull. But when you tried, something would be wrong. (Act as though you are pulling from the other side.) Only when you look do you realize that the door has a different message on the other side. (Show it.) See, on this side it says push to open. But on the other side it says pull. You have to know which side of the door you are on. The signs are there to help you.

The Bible reading for today also shows us two sides of something. The story is about the birth of Jesus. Some men who studied the stars saw a sign in the sky that told them the Savior of the world had been born. They were happy to see Jesus. They came to worship Him. They brought Him gifts. They thought the birth of Jesus was the best thing that ever happened to the world.

But the Bible reading also tells us about some other people

who heard that Jesus was born. When King Herod learned that another king had been born, he was upset. When he told other people about what he thought was a problem, they were upset too.

The Wise Men and Herod are like people who came to the same door, but from different sides. One saw Jesus and the door opened—everything was great. The other found out about Jesus and the door was closed. They were angry and frustrated. For them it was bad news.

Herod's problem was not that he was on the wrong side of Jesus. Jesus has no bad side. Herod made the mistake of not reading the sign.

Jesus is like this door. When we come to Him from the side of our sin, we see a sign that says, "Repent." (Show second door.) When we repent, we can go through the door. From the other side the door says, "Believe." (Show it.) After you have repented, believe that Christ has forgiven your sin. Believe that He is your Savior. Be like the Wise Men. Worship Him. Give Him gifts. Love Him. Be happy about having seen Him.

But when you find yourself banging against the door and it won't open, when you want to pray but can't or you feel God isn't listening; stop and take a look at the signs. Sometimes when we see Jesus we need to repent and receive the forgiveness He gives. At other times we need to worship Him and use that forgiveness to forgive and help others. If you feel separated from God, then see the sign that says repent. If you know you are forgiven, see the sign that says beleive. Then you know that Christ lives with you. And you with Him.

The Gift You Can't Put Away

The Word

At that time Jesus went from Galilee to the Jordan, and came to John to be baptized by him. But John tried to make Him change His mind. "I ought to be baptized by You," John said, "yet You come to me!" But Jesus answered him, "Let it be so for now. For in this way we shall do all that God requires." So John agreed. Matthew 3:13-15 (From the Gospel for the First Sunday After Epiphany)

The World

A Christmas decoration and the box in which it was purchased and a child's toy that would have come in a box which would not be kept for storage.

Let me show you two Christmas gifts. This gift (a manger scene) was used during the holidays. But now it is back in the box that it came in. The gift will be put away until next Christmas. This gift (a doll) also came in a box. It was wrapped as a present and placed under the tree. But the box was thrown away. The doll is to be played with every day; so you would not keep the box.

Now let's ask about the most important gift that you received at Christmas. God's gift to you was His Son, a Baby wrapped in blankets and laid in a manger. Is that gift like this one (manger scene)? one that you will put back in the box and keep for next Christmas? Or is the gift of Jesus like this gift (doll)? one that will be used every day?

In our Bible reading we hear about John, the man God sent to prepare the world for Jesus. When Jesus asked John to baptize Him, John said that it should be the other way around. John knew that Jesus came to save all people. That meant that Jesus had to take our place. But when Jesus asked to be baptized, John said no. John wanted to keep Jesus for some

27

special event. He wanted to put Him away to be used later.

Do we do the same thing? When Jesus tells us that He is with us always, do we think, "No, He is too busy for us. He can wait and be with us when we have a big problem"? Do we put Him in a box for later? When He tells us to love our neighbor, do we say, "Later on, Lord. Stay in Your box until I need You"? When He tells us to forgive others, do we say, "not now"?

You may think of other ways that we try to put Jesus in a box. Any time you tell Jesus that you will do what He says later you are putting Him away. But Jesus explained to John that they must do what God asked them to do. And the Bible says "John agreed." That's a beautiful thought: John agreed. Could we write your name in that sentence? Jerry agreed. Cindy agreed. Linda agreed.

Then when John baptized Jesus, he saw the heavens open. And he heard God say, "This is My own dear Son, with whom I am well pleased." When we use God's gift to us every day, we also hear God speak to us. He tells us how He loves us. He guides and protects us. Don't put Jesus in a box. Don't keep Him stored away to be used later. He has something for you now. When you were baptized in His name, He became a part of your daily life.

Find Out Who Jesus Is—and Was

The Word

The next day John saw Jesus coming to him and said: "Here is the Lamb of God who takes away the sin of the world! This is the One I was talking about when I said, 'A Man is coming after me, but He is greater than I am, because He existed before I was born.'" John 1:29-30 (From the Gospel for the Second Sunday After Epiphany)

The World

Paper airplanes made from a piece of typing paper, a page out of a magazine, a piece of junk mail, a dollar bill.

Which of these paper airplanes would you rather have? First take a look at them. You can see that they are different sizes and shapes. To see which one is the best airplane we must also fly them (do it). See—some fly better than others. If I offered you one of the paper airplanes, which would you take?

I think all of you would take this one (dollar bill). Maybe this plane doesn't fly as well as the others, but you may have noticed that it is made from a dollar bill. It is a paper airplane now, but before I folded it, it was a dollar bill. And when I unfold it (do it), it is still a dollar bill.

Now remember the paper airplanes as we talk about the Bible reading for today. John the Baptist speaks to the people who lived at his time and also to us when he says, "Here is the Lamb of God who takes away the sin of the world." John wanted all people to follow Jesus. He tells us there is something special about Jesus.

But the people who saw Jesus could not see that He was special. Jesus was not as rich as many others. He was not an important person in the government or church. His family was not important in the community. If the people had to choose

29

the most important man they knew, they would not have picked Jesus.

But John told them that Jesus was the greatest because He existed before any of them. The lives of all people start when they are born. But Jesus was always God. And He became also a human being. Jesus can be the Lamb of God that takes away the sin of the world because He is God who also became a man. He is like the paper airplane made from a dollar bill. What He was before He became a person is important.

John tells us to follow Jesus. When we see what Jesus tells us to do, we might say we would rather follow someone else. Jesus leads us to places where we serve others. But someone else might lead us to be rich and famous. But before you make your choice, remember the paper airplanes. This (the dollar bill) didn't make the best airplaine; yet it is worth way more than the others. Because Jesus is God who came to earth to be our Savior, He can lead us not only through this life but He also leads us to eternal life. Follow Him.

Be a Waiter or Waitress

The Word

As Jesus walked by Lake Galilee, He saw two brothers who were fishermen, Simon (called Peter) and his brother Andrew, catching fish in the lake with a net. Jesus said to them, "Come with Me and I will teach you to catch men." At once they left their nets and went with Him. Matthew 4:18-20 (From the Gospel for the Third Sunday After Epiphany)

The World

A container for an individual serving and a barrel for a larger amount of fried chicken from a drive-in restaurant.

When Jesus asked fishermen to work for Him, He told them they would be fishers of men. Instead of catching fish for food, they would bring people to know salvation through Christ. Since we are not fishermen, let's pretend that Jesus speaks to us and imagine how He would ask us to serve Him.

All of us eat. Most of us have eaten at a fried chicken restaurant. We would like to have the food that comes in a barrel like this. In the restaurant the cook fills the barrel with chicken and the waiter brings it to us. Now think about what God gives to us. He fills the barrel with love and forgiveness. When Jesus came to live for us, He put perfect obedience into the barrel for us. He died for our sins; so He filled the barrel with forgiveness. He put grace and understanding into the barrel for us. God is like the cook at the restaurant. He provides the food. He offers it to us. We receive what He gives.

But notice that Jesus offers us a barrel full of His gifts. He did not give His love to us in a small container like this. This is for an individual serving. If you received it you would have only enough for yourself. Instead, Jesus gives you His gifts in a barrel. After you have had all you need, and even more than

31

you need, the barrel is not empty. You have love, forgiveness, mercy, and all the other gifts of God left over to give to others.

You need to know when you need to receive the gifts that God has. Look at your own life and see who is the waiter or waitress that serves you with the message of God's mercy in Jesus Christ. Continue to receive that gift.

But when you receive it, remember that you can also give it to others. Think about the many people you know who need to learn about Jesus for the first time or who need to grow in faith toward Him. Then hear Jesus call you to be a waiter or a waitress. You are to hand the barrel containing His love and grace to others. Maybe some will not take it because they think they don't need it. Then you must show them why they need Christ's help. Others will not take it because they are afraid they can't afford it. Then you must show them that it is free. But many will be glad to receive the gift that God has given to you.

Jesus calls you to be His disciple. As He gives you gifts for your own life He also gives you extra gifts to give to others.

Happiness Is a Shadow

The Word

(If possible, print the text, as shown below, in the bulletin or an insert so worshipers may join in reading it responsively.)

A	B
Happy are those who know they are spiritually poor;	THE KINGDOM OF HEAVEN BELONGS TO THEM!
Happy are those who mourn;	GOD WILL COMFORT THEM!
Happy are the meek;	THEY WILL RECEIVE WHAT GOD HAS PROMISED!
Happy are those whose greatest desire is to do what God requires;	GOD WILL SATISFY THEM FULLY!
Happy are those who are merciful to others;	GOD WILL BE MERCIFUL TO THEM!
Happy are the pure in heart;	THEY WILL SEE GOD!
Happy are those who work for peace among men;	GOD WILL CALL THEM HIS SONS!
Happy are those who are persecuted because they do what God requires;	THE KINGDOM OF HEAVEN BELONGS TO THEM!

Matthew 5:3-10 (From the Gospel for the Fourth Sunday After Epiphany)

The World

An overhead projector.

When our Bible reading is divided into two parts, it gives us a choice. Would you rather have the first column? Or the second? (If the text cannot be printed for all, read it in two parts as printed above.)

The first part promises us that we will be happy. But it also says we will be spiritually poor, that we will mourn, be meek, and must do what God want us to do. It tells us to be pure in heart, merciful, and to work for peace. Finally, it says we will be persecuted. Sometimes we don't want the gifts listed in the first column.

Now look at the second column. It says the kingdom of heaven belongs to us. God comforts us. We will receive what God has promised. He will satisfy us fully. God will be merciful to us. We will see God. He will call us to be His children, and the kingdom of heaven belongs to us. We like that list. If we had our choice, we would take the gifts under *B*.

But Jesus is telling us that we can't have *B* without *A*. Notice that the happiness is connected with the *A* lists. By facing the struggles described in the first column, we are happy because we receive the blessings in the second.

You could look at it this way. (Turn on the projector with the lights shining on a wall.) The gifts in column B are like a shadow. (Hold your hand in front of the projector to make a shadow.) But the problems mentioned in column A are like my hand. I can't make the shadow on the wall without putting my hand in front of the light. You can't get the happiness that God wants to give you unless you take it the way God gives it. Happiness is the shadow caused by giving something else. You can't look for happiness by itself. You must do something else and you will receive happiness.

We see this in the life of Jesus. He gives us happiness. We have happiness because He has promised us eternal life. We have happiness because He loves us and is with us. But those gifts are like shadows on the wall. They are real only because He died on the cross to make them possible.

If you want to be happy, look for ways to serve God and other people. By helping others you will cast a shadow of happiness for yourself and for others.

Pass the Salt

The Word

Jesus said, "You are like salt for all mankind. But if salt loses its taste, there is no way to make it salty again. It has become worthless, so it is thrown away and people walk on it." Matthew 5:13 (From the Gospel for the Fifth Sunday After Epiphany)

The World

A saltshaker filled with salt.

Jesus did not tell us that we should be salt. Or that we will be salt. He said we are salt. Salt adds to the flavor of food and makes it taste better. Jesus has given us love and other spiritual gifts that make us like salt for other people. We can add to their lives and make them better.

But Jesus also says that we might lose our salty flavor. In our time we cannot imagine how salt can lose its flavor. But remember that the salt that Jesus used didn't come from a grocery store. Salt was scraped up from dried up ponds that had been filled with saltwater. When the water evaporated, the salt was left on the bottom of the pond. But the salt also included sand and other things. If the salt got wet and dissolved, only the sand was left. So the salt had lost its flavor. Today Jesus might say, "You are like a saltshaker (show the shaker); but if a saltshaker is empty, there is no way for it to salt anything."

Jesus asks us to see if we are salt for other people. Remember, we add salt to the lives of others when we share the love, understanding, kindness, mercy, hope, joy, and many other happy blessings that God has given us in Jesus. Now look at yourself and see if you sprinkle those things into the lives of others.

First, listen to the words that you say. Do your words help

other people? Are they salt that makes other people happy? Start by thinking how you talk to other members of your family. What do you say when you get up in the morning? When you come home from school? When you are eating with your family? Now think about the things you say at school to friends and to teachers. Think of how you talk to people who work in stores, who clean your school, or drive your bus. Are the words you say salt for the lives of others? Do you make other people better by what you say? Do they receive a flavor from what you say?

Now think about the way you act with other people? Do you smile to others? Are you friendly and polite? Do you treat people as though you believe that God made each of them and that He sent His Son to be the Savior for each of them? Are you concerned about other people's problems, and are you glad when others have something nice happen to them? Do you add something good to the lives of others?

If sometimes you think you are an empty shaker, then remember how you can be the salt of the earth. The salt comes from Jesus. He gives us the love to others. He gives us the good flavor of joy and mercy so we can share it with others.

Think of yourself as a saltshaker in your family, your school, your neighborhood. Jesus tells you to pass the salt. He puts you near others. Let Christ's love sprinkle on them through you.

Cut Off Whose Hand?

The Word

Jesus said, "If your right hand causes you to sin, cut it off and throw it away! It is much better for you to lose one of your limbs than to have your whole body go off to hell." Matthew 5:30 (From the Gospel for the Sixth Sunday After Epiphany)

The World

The figure of a clown cut from paper (large enough to be easily seen from the last pew), an extra hand (but the same size as the first) taped over the right hand of the clown with a straight pin stuck through the hand (point out), several balloons already blown up.

Suppose we were using this clown as a party decoration and wanted a balloon in his hand. I'll tie the balloon to his wrist (as you do it, press the balloon against the pin). I broke the balloon; so I'll use another (repeat). Here's the problem. See, the hand has a pin in it. Each balloon will break when it hits the pin.

In our Bible reading today Jesus reminds us that we often repeat the same sins over and over again. We not only tell a lie, but we repeat the same lie many times. We not only say words that hurt others, but we continue to use those same words. We continue to feel the same hate, lust, greed. Each time we repeat our sins, we hurt ourselves and others.

Jesus tells us, "If your right hand causes you to sin, cut it off and throw it away! It is better for you to lose one of your limbs than to have your whole body go off to hell."

Jesus' words scare us at first. Does He mean for us to hurt our own bodies? If we stole something with our hand, would He want us to lose the hand? If we said words that hurt others would He want us to cut off our tongue? That seems like a bad way to solve a problem. Yet think about the clown. I can't keep on putting balloons on the hand and have the pin break them. It is foolish to keep on repeating the same mistake.

When Jesus tells us to cut off our hand if we sin, He is reminding us that sin causes pain and suffering. He does not want us to wait until we die to find out about the punishment. He warns us now so we can escape the punishment.

Look at the clown. We can cut off the hand that caused the problem. See (remove the extra hand with the pin). Now I can put a balloon on the wrist and it won't break.

But the clown had an extra hand. You and I don't—we don't unless we remember that Jesus put Himself in our place to pay the price of sin. Some think Jesus was cruel when He asked us to cut off our hand if we sin. But remember, He not only gave the punishment, He also took the punishment. He gave Himself, His hand, His eyes, His tongue, as a sacrifice for us.

Now when we sin, He asks us to remember His sacrifice. Remember that His resurrection gives us a new life. He helps free us from sin. We still have to struggle against evil, but Jesus is on our side. We don't have to repeat the same mistakes over and over. He removes the problem and gives us a new way to live.

My Way—or Your Way?

The Word

Jesus said, "You have heard that it was said, 'Love your friends, hate your enemies.' But I tell you: Love your enemies, and pray for those who persecute you, so that you will become the sons of your Father in heaven." Matthew 5:43-45 (From the Gospel for the Seventh Sunday After Epiphany)

The World

On a tray: box of tea bags, several glasses, spoon, teacup, pitcher of water, thermos of hot water.

If your father liked to drink tea and you wanted to do something nice for him, you might decide to make some tea for him. Making tea is easy. All you need is tea and water. See: (Pour water from the pitcher in the glass. Tear open a tea bag and dump the tea leaves into the glass. Stir). But something's wrong with this tea. It looks bad. I don't even want to taste it. So I'll try again. (Repeat as before.) This isn't right either.

If I keep on trying to make tea the wrong way, it will never turn out right. If I want to change the way the tea tastes, I have to change the way I make it. See: (Pour hot water into the cup. Put the tea bag into the water. Show how the water becomes tea). Now this is a good cup of tea.

Remember the problem of making tea as you think about the way you live with other people. You want to do good things for God and other people. But sometimes what you do doesn't turn out right. If you intend to play and have fun but instead fight and argue with others, something is wrong. If you go to Sunday school or church to learn about God, but instead you get into trouble for misbehaving or you daydream and don't hear God's Word, something is wrong.

When something you try to do doesn't turn out right, you

can't start over again and repeat it the same way. If you keep on doing something the wrong way, you will never improve. If you want to change what happens, you have to change the way you live—just as I had to change the way I made tea if I wanted the tea to taste good.

Jesus says that many people say, "Love your friends, hate your enemies." But if you follow that advice you will always have trouble. If you argue and get angry, if you fight and disagree, or if you try to get even with others, you will always make enemies. You may be sorry that you made the enemies; but unless you change your attitude about people, you will continue to make more enemies.

Jesus gives us a way to change. He says, "But I tell you: Love your enemies, and pray for those who persecute you, so that you will become the sons of your Father in heaven." Jesus gives us a new way to live with people. He says to treat all people with love and respect. Jesus didn't just talk about love. He did love His enemies. He asked God to forgive those who killed Him. He forgives the sins of all people. He wants to help all people. He helps us today, not because we are good and deserve His love, but because He is good and gives us His love.

When you find yourself having trouble with others, ask: Am I treating people my way? Or am I treating them the same way Jesus would treat them? Change your way to follow His way.

God: to Have or to Serve

The Word

Jesus said, "No one can be a slave to two masters; he will hate one and love the other; he will be loyal to one and despise the other. You cannot serve both God and money." Matthew 6:24 (From the Gospel for the Eighth Sunday After Epiphany)

The World

A chalkboard or large poster on which you have written an addition problem that would be difficult for the children present.

You are taking a test in math class at school. This is one of the problems. As you add the number the first time, you come up with this answer. (Write an answer that is incorrect, but close to the right answer.) Then to check yourself you add the numbers again and come up with this answer. (Write the correct answer under the first.)

Now you have two answers for the test. If you worked the problem again you might even come up with another answer. But the addition of these numbers can have only one correct answer. When you hand your paper to the teahcer, you have to know which answer is the right one. You can have two answers only until the time comes when you must depend on one or the other. Then you must decide which answer you will trust to get you a good grade.

Jesus tells us we have the same choice regarding God and money. Often we come up with two different answers when we ask how we can solve the problems in our lives. Sometimes we say God is the answer. And sometimes we say money is the answer.

Just as we can have two answers to the same math problem, we can have both God and money in our lives. But we will also

41

have to face a time when we must choose between the two. We can have both God and money, but we cannot depend on both God and money.

We depend on money for some things—to buy our food, pay our medical bills, give us a good time. But money can do only so much for us. First, we have only so much money. When it's gone, it's gone. Second, even if we have lots of money, it can only do certain things. It can pay for medicine, but it can't guarantee you that you will live. Money can pay for a good time, but not guarantee that you'll have a good time. If you have money, you use it. That's good. God gave you money to use.

But if you depend on money, you serve it. That is not good. God wants you to serve Him. If you are serving money, you cannot be serving God. If you are depending on money, you cannot be depending on God.

So Jesus asks you to make a choice. Don't wait until you have to hand the test in on Judgment Day, but make the choice now. Do you want to have God and have money too—like having two answers to one math problem? Or do you want to serve God? Do you want to depend on Him for everything, both now and forever?

As you make your choice, remember what God has done for you. He sent Jesus to be your Savior. Jesus gave His life for you. He served you so you can serve Him. Don't just have a Savior. Serve your Savior.

The Light Is On

The Word

As they [Peter, James, and John] looked on; a change came over Him [Jesus]: His face became as bright as the sun, and His clothes as white as light. . . . While he was talking, a shining cloud came over them, and a voice said from the cloud: "This is My own dear Son, with whom I am well pleased—listen to Him." Matthew 17:2, 5 (From the Gospel for the Last Sunday After Epiphany)

The World

A traffic light—made by cutting two circles from a piece of cardboard and covering the holes with red and green opaque paper, a flashlight.

When you are riding your bike and see a traffic light like this, you might ride right past it without paying any attention. The light doesn't tell you what to do when both lights are turned off. But when one of the lights is on (shine flashlight behind the green paper), it tells you whether you should stop or go. The message is important for your life.

When Jesus lived as a person on this earth, many people also walked right past Him. He did not look different than other people. His appearance did not make people stop to listen to Him. Then one day He was on a mountain with three of His disciples. His appearance changed. The disciples who had seen Him many times saw that He looked different. Before, they had seen Him as a person. But now they also saw Him as God. They also heard the voice of God say, "This is My own dear Son, with whom I am well pleased—listen to Him."

Before the day of His transfiguration (that's what we call the time that His appearance changed) Jesus had been like the traffic signal when the lights were turned off. Then the disciples saw Him with the lights turned on. They saw Him as God's Son.

God the Father told them to follow Jesus. When Jesus told them to stop mistreating people, to stop saying bad things, they knew that God was speaking to them. When Jesus told them to go to the world with the message of His love for all people, to go to others who needed help, they knew that God was telling them to go.

Sometimes we forget that we have seen the light in Jesus. We get used to knowing that we are baptized, and we forget to remember the power that Jesus gives us in our baptism. We get used to having our Bibles around and forget that Jesus comes to us in the Scripture. That's why we need to see the lights in Jesus. We need to know that He speaks for God in our lives. We need to hear God tell us when to stop and when to go.

You can be like Peter, James, and John. You can see the beauty of Christ in our life. Listen to His Word. Read His Word. See the lights shine in your life.

Your Defense Against Temptation

The Word

Then the devil took Jesus to a very high mountain and showed Him all the kingdoms of the world, in all their greatness. "All this I will give You," the devil said, "if You kneel down and worship me." Then Jesus answered, "Go away, Satan! The Scripture says, 'Worship the Lord your God and serve only Him!'" Matthew 4:8-10 (From the Gospel for the First Sunday in Lent)

The World

A ballpoint pen, a stack of typing paper, a picture of a child.

The Bible story for today tells about part of the battle between Jesus and Satan. First Satan attacks. He offers Jesus great wealth and power. He says, "I will give You all the kingdoms of the world if You kneel down and worship me."

Then we read how Jesus defended Himself from the temptation. He did not argue with Satan. He didn't mention that the devil could not give Him the land that He already owned. He didn't ask questions about the value of the kingdoms. Instead Jesus used God's Word to defend Himself. He said, "The Scripture says, 'Worship the Lord your God and serve only Him!'"

We are also tempted by Satan. And we also have God's Word to defend ourselves. We need to look at the things that tempt us so we know how to defend ourselves.

Let's pretend this (picture of a child) is you. And this ballpoint pen will be the devil's temptation. See how the devil wants to change you (put the pen on the picture). He wants to make you look like his person instead of God's person. So you need protection. If you put this (one sheet of paper) over the picture the pen can't mark it. Just as God's Word was Jesus' defense against Satan's temptation, the paper is the picture's protection from the pen. But if the pen bears down hard (do it), it can mark through the paper and still change the picture. So you need more protection. (Add a stack of paper to the picture.) Now the pen cannot hurt the picture. The paper is thick enough to stop the pen. The harder the pen is pushed, the more paper is needed to protect the picture.

And the more temptations you have, the more you need the Word of God to protect you. The devil wants to change you by making you lie, cheat, and hurt people. And you need protection from the temptation.

It is not the paper in the Bible that protects you, but the message of Christ. God's Word tells you that Christ has been tempted in every way that you are tempted. When we are tempted, we sometimes sin. But Jesus never did. Yet He died for sin—not His sin but ours.

Now He helps us two ways. When we are tempted and do sin, He forgives us. He also protects us from temptation. He is like the thick stack of paper that protected the picture. Sin always hurts us and He wants to protect us. Know when you are tempted, and use the power that God gives you in Jesus to protect yourself.

What Holds You to Jesus?

The Word

Many of the Samaritans in the town believed in Jesus because the woman had said, "He told me everything I have ever done." So when the Samaritans came to Him, they begged Him to stay with them; and Jesus stayed there two days. Many more believed because of His message, and they told the woman, "We believe now, not because of what you said, but because we ourselves have heard Him and we know that He is really the Savior of the world." John 4:39-41 (From the context of the Gospel for the Second Sunday in Lent)

The World

Two blocks of wood, glue, string.

Jesus met a women at a well in Samaria and told her many things about her life. He also told her He was the Savior God has promised for the world. The woman ran to her village and told other people.

Because Jesus knew things about the woman that no stranger could have known, they were curious. They went out to listen to Jesus. Then they asked Him to stay with them. They believed that Jesus was the Savior that they had read about in the Old Testament. They told the woman, "We believe now, not because of what you said, but because we ourselves have heard Him, and we know that He is really the Savior of the world."

This story tells us how we are to know Jesus as our Savior and how we can share Him with others. Pretend this block is Jesus. And this one is you. For you to know Jesus as your Savior you must come to Him and stay with Him. (Put the two blocks together.) But something has to hold you close to Jesus. That something is the Holy Spirit. We'll use this glue to represent God's Spirit. The glue must be on the block that represents Jesus because the Spirit uses Christ's death and resurrection in our place to bring us to faith. (Put glue on one side of the Jesus block.) Now you and Jesus can stick together. (Do it.) But the blocks won't stay together. (Pull them apart.) The glue has to dry before it can hold the two blocks together. So I must put string around the blocks to hold them together. (Do it.) Now the string will keep the two blocks together until the glue dries. Then we can take the string off, and the blocks will stay together.

The woman at the well was like the string. She held Jesus and the people from the village together for a short time. Then after the people heard the message of Jesus they believed in Him. At first their faith depended upon the woman's message. Then it depended upon Jesus.

Your parents, pastor, teachers, and friends are like the string for you. We want to bring you close to Jesus. But our help is only temporary. We want you to believe in Jesus, not because we told you to, but because you know He loves you and gave Himself for you.

You can also be string for other people. You can bring someone to Jesus. For a while they will depend on you to keep them close to the Savior. Then they will believe for themselves.

A New Way to See

The Word

Jesus said, "I came to this world to judge, so that the blind should see, and those who see should become blind." John 9:39 (From the Gospel for the Third Sunday in Lent)

The World

A large box with "Romans 3:28" written on the inside so a person with the box over his head could read it, and a poster with "Ephesians 2:8" written on it.

In our Bible reading Jesus talks about those who are blind and those who can see. To help us understand what He said I need two children (choose fourth- or fifth-graders) to help me. Mary, I'll ask you to represent blind people. To make it real I'll put this box over your head so you can't see. (Do it with the writing to her back so she cannot see it.) Dennis, you will represent the people who can see.

Jesus said, "I came to the world to judge, so that the blind should see, and those who see should become blind." Jesus tells us He will come to judge us. And He says His judgment is going to make things different than they seem to be now.

For example, we know that blind people can't see. I don't have to prove that, but let's do it just to show how the judgment will work. I am going to read a verse from the Bible and show a card that tells where the words can be found. Only those who can see will be able to read the card. Okay: "For it is by God's grace that you have been saved, through faith. It is not your own doing, but God's gift." (Show the Eph. 2:8 poster. Point out that the person who can see can read the answer but the other cannot.)

That is how we think the judgment would be. But Jesus says

that the blind will be able to see and those who can see will be like those who are blind. I know that sounds backwards. But let's try again. I'll read another sentence from the Bible. "For we conclude that a man is put right with God only through faith, and not by doing what the Law commands." Again I will show the answer. (Turn the box around so the person it can see the answer. Help her read the answer, and point out that the other person cannot read it.) This time the person who could not see had the advantage because the answer was inside the box. The same box that kept her from seeing everything else helped her see the answer. But Dennis could see everything else and couldn't see what was in the box.

When Jesus judges us, things will also be reversed. If we think we can see the answers and save ourselves by our own good works, we will be like one who is blind. But if we know we are blind and recognize that we need help, we will see the answer. The answer is that Christ loves us and came to earth to be our Savior before He came to be our Judge.

During this Lenten season, we want to see how our sin makes us blind. We cannot see God. But Jesus came inside our sinful world and shared our blindness with us. Because He is in the box with us, we can see the answer. If we think we don't need Him, we are outside the box and can't see the answer.

Are You to Be Seen? Or to Serve?

The Word

Jesus said, "If one of you wants to be great, he must be the servant of the rest; and if one of you wants to be first, he must be your slave—like the Son of Man, who did not come to be served, but to serve and to give His life to redeem many people." Matthew 20:26b-28 (From the Gospel for the Fourth Sunday in Lent)

The World

An apple that is slightly spotted or wrinkled and an artificial apple.

If I offered you one of these apples, which would you take? This one (artificial) is prettier. If you wanted the apple to decorate your table, you would take it. Notice the other is spotty and wrinkled. The first looks better.

But if you were hungry, you'd take the one that doesn't look as good. You could cut out the spots and eat it. But this good-looking apple could not be eaten because it is made from plastic.

So if you had your choice of the two apples, you would first have to decide why you wanted an apple. If you only wanted to look at it, take this one. If you wanted to eat it—take this one.

Some of Jesus' disciples asked Him to choose them to sit beside Him in heaven. They wanted the special honor of being seen with Jesus. But Jesus said, "If one of you wants to be great, he must be the servant of the rest; and if one of you wants to be first, he must be your slave—like the Son of Man, who did not come to be served, but to serve and to give His life to redeem many people."

The disciples wanted to look great in the eyes of others. They wanted to be a decoration—like the apple. But Jesus said that people are not meant to be decorations. We are not great

51

because we make others look at us and give us special honors.

Instead, He says we are great when we are willing to serve others. As the apple was made to be eaten, we were made to live with and to help other people. Sometimes we think we can't help others. We may feel we have nothing to offer. But others do need us. This apple may not be pretty. But if you were hungry, you would enjoy it. Even with your faults, other people need you.

Jesus reminds us that we can help others even though we ourselves also need help. He says we are to be like Him. He came not to be served but to serve and to give His life to redeem us. Because He has served us and has forgiven our sins, He has cut out the bad spots of our lives. He has made us His people so we can also serve others.

How to Save By Throwing Away

The Word

One of them, named Caiaphas, who was high priest that year, said, "You do not know a thing! Don't you realize that it is better for you to have one man die for the people, instead of the whole nation being destroyed?" John 11:49-50 (From the Gospel for the Fifth Sunday in Lent)

The World

A small box of tomatoes, including one that is badly bruised.

When Jesus raised His friend Lazarus from the dead, many people were happy. But others became angry. The religious leaders of the day knew that more and more people were following Jesus. From their point of view Jesus was destroying their religion. So they held a meeting. Some said that Jesus would get all the people to believe in Him and no one would come to their temple anymore.

But Caiaphas, the high priest, said, "You don't know a thing! Don't you realize that it is better for you to have one man die for the people, instead of the whole nation being destroyed?" Caiaphas was a practical person. If Jesus was a problem, he said get rid of Jesus.

To understand Caiaphas' idea, look at this box of tomatoes. The tomatoes are all in good condition except this one. It is bruised. The skin is broken. The juice will run out on the other tomatoes and ruin them too if it stays in the box. So protect the good tomatoes, I will throw this one away. Caiaphas felt the same way about Jesus. Get rid of Him before His ideas mess up others.

Now let's go back to the tomatoes. I threw the bad one out in the flower garden. The others stayed in the refrigerator until they were eaten. The seeds from the spoiled tomato settled down into the ground. Plants grew from the seeds and produced many more tomatoes. Think about what happened. The one tomato that I threw away grew to make many tomatoes. But those in the box were eaten. By throwing out the bruised tomato, I intended to save those in the box. Instead, I saved many more tomatoes because they grew from the seeds of the tomato that was tossed out into the yard.

Without intending to, Caiaphas also spoke of saving many people when He said, "Don't you realize that it is better for you to have one man die for the people, instead of the whole nation being destroyed?" He meant to say that if they killed Jesus, He wouldn't bother them anymore. But what really happened was that Jesus died as a sacrifice that saved many people. Caiaphas wanted only to save the few people in Jerusalem from Jesus' teachings. But when Jesus was killed on the cross, He became the Savior of the world. After His death He arose again, and He also will raise us from the dead. Like the seeds growing from the tomato that was tossed out produced many more tomatoes, the new life in Christ is shared with many people as others also die and will be raised again.

As you think about Jesus' death, remember that He died for you. Because He was tossed out, you are saved.

If You Don't Know, Ask

The Word

When Jesus entered Jerusalem, the whole city was thrown in an uproar. "Who is He?" the people asked. "This is the prophet Jesus, from Nazareth of Galilee," the crowds answered. Matthew 21:10-11 (From the Gospel for Palm Sunday)

The World

A carton of eggs and a carton of eggs decorated for Easter.

Think how often you put a carton of eggs like this (plain eggs) in the refrigerator and then take the eggs out as you use them. Eggs are a routine part of life for most people, and we use them without paying much attention to what they look like.

But suppose one morning this week that you went to the refrigerator and when you opened the carton you saw eggs like this (decorated eggs). These eggs are different. You know they are not intended for your breakfast.

You would probably know why these special eggs were in your refrigerator. Next Sunday is Easter and you know that people decorate eggs for Easter. But if you didn't know about Easter and hadn't heard about dyeing eggs, you would wonder what kind of a chicken would lay such eggs. You'd have to ask where the eggs came from.

We can use these eggs to help understand how the people in Jesusalem saw Jesus on the first Palm Sunday. Jesus had gone in and out of Jerusalem many times in His life. His first trip was when He was a baby. On Palm Sunday He came back to Jerusalem to die. On His other trips to the holy city few people noticed Him. He was like the carton of plain eggs. He was a part of the lives of people.

But on Palm Sunday He entered Jerusalem in a different

way. Crowds of people came to greet Him. The children sang praises to God for Him. People put down palm branches and coats on the ground to make a path for Him. Jesus had become special to many people. He was like the carton of brightly decorated eggs.

But not all of the people of Jerusalem knew that Jesus was so special. Our Bible reading says that some asked, "Who is He?" But others knew the answer. They said, "This is the prophet Jesus, from Nazareth of Galilee."

As we celebrate Easter this year, we will have eggs, candy, and new clothes. In the middle of all the decorations will also be pictures of Jesus, and we will hear the words He said. Some will have to ask, "Who is He?" Others will answer, "He is the Savior of the world, who died to take away all our sin and who rose from the dead."

Will you be one who asks the question or one who gives the answer? If you don't know who Jesus is, ask. And listen to the answer. If you do know, listen for others to ask about Him and be ready to give an answer.

Know Where to Look for the Answer

The Word

Then the other disciple, who had reached the tomb first, also went in; he saw and believed. (They still did not understand the Scripture which said that He must rise from death.) John 20:8-9 (From the Easter Gospel)

The World

A can of chicken noodle soup, another can of chicken noodle soup with the label removed but with "Chicken Noodle" written on the bottom, a can opener.

On the first Easter morning Peter and John heard that the stone had been rolled away from Jesus' grave. They rushed to the cemetery. Our Bible reading tells us that after they went into the tomb and saw the empty grave-clothes, they believed that Jesus had risen from the dead. But then John, who was one of those two disciples to visit the grave and who also wrote our Bible lesson, adds, "They still did not understand the Scripture which said that He must rise from death."

The two disciples had to see the empty grave before they could believe that Jesus was alive again. But John knew that people like us who would live many years later could not see the empty grave. So he reminds us that the Bible tells us that Jesus still lives just as clearly as the empty tomb did.

Let's use an illustration. If you had this can (without a label), you would not know what was in it. One way to find out would be to open it (do it). Now we can see that the can is filled with chicken noodle soup. We have seen it. Peter and John also had to look into the tomb to see that it was empty.

But if I had looked at the bottom of the can (show it by holding the can up), I would not have had to open it. See, it says "Chicken Noodle" on the bottom. If Peter and John had remembered the Old Testament prophecies about Christ, they would have known that Jesus was to rise from the dead. They would have believed the written message rather than having to see for themselves.

You and I have even more than the Old Testament promises. We also have the New Testament that tells us over and over again that Jesus who died also rose from the dead. We don't have to look for a hidden message under the can. Instead, the message is clear—like on this can (with the label). You know what is in the can. The message about Christ is also clear for us today. He rose from the dead.

The most important part of Easter for you is that you know that Jesus Christ did return from the dead and that His new life is shared with you. Because He lives after He had died, you also can survive death. You also will live again.

Because the message is so important, we all want proof that it is true. Remember the Bible reading. The one who wrote it saw the empty tomb, and later he also saw the living Christ. But even though he was an eyewitness to the resurrection, John tells us to look to the Bible for proof. That same message is for us today. It tells us that Jesus is alive.

Peace Be with You

The Word

It was late that Sunday evening, and the disciples were gathered together behind locked doors, because they were afraid of the Jewish authorities. Then Jesus came and stood among them. "Peace be with you," He said. John 20:19 (From the Gospel for the Second Sunday of Easter).

The World

Four posters (or transparencies for an overhead projector) with the following messages: "You failed me." "I told you so." "I'll give you one more chance." "Peace be with you."

The first Easter Sunday was a rough day for the disciples who had followed Jesus during His ministry on earth. They had seen Jesus killed on a cross three days before. They were afraid that as soon as the religious holiday was over the religious leaders would look for them and kill them too. Then on Easter morning the women told them that Jesus' tomb was empty and that an angel had said He was alive again.

That evening the disciples were in a locked room to hide from the authorities when Jesus appeared in the room with them. You can imagine how afraid they were. They locked the door to keep the soldiers out. But they couldn't hide from Jesus behind a locked door. They remembered how they had deserted Him—how they had failed Him when He needed them. You can imagine how afraid they were. What would Jesus say to them? How would He treat them after they had failed Him?

Let's think of some of the things that Jesus might have said to the disciples. He could have told them, "You failed me." (Show words.) He could have reminded the disciples that they ran away when He was arrested and that only one of them came to the hill where He was crucified.

Or He could have said, "I told you so." He had told the disciples that they would leave Him. But they all had insisted that they would never go away from Him. He could have reminded them that He had warned them but they would not listen.

Or Jesus could have said, "I'll give you one more chance." I'm sure the disciples would have promised to do better the next time. But they had made those kinds of promises before.

However, Jesus said none of those things. Do you know what He did say? He said, "Peace be with you." He did not come back to scold them, to remind them of their failures, or even to give them another chance. He came back to give them peace. He had earned peace for them when He died on the cross in their place. He came back to show them that He loved them and they could have peace with God and with one another.

Jesus also has the same message for you. Peace be with you. Jesus did not return from the dead to continue the battle against sin. He has already won that battle when He died and came back to life again. Because He has destroyed sin's power to send us to hell, He has given us peace.

Peace be with you.

Remember Your Past and Your Future

The Word

Then Jesus said to them, "How foolish you are, how slow you are to believe everything the prophets said! Was it not necessary for the Messiah to suffer these things and enter His glory?" And Jesus explained to them what was said about Him in all the Scriptures, beginning with the books of Moses and the writings of all the prophets. Luke 24:25-27 (From the Gospel for the Third Sunday of Easter)

The World

A large road map of your state and an inch wide strip cut from across the middle of another map exactly like the first.

Could you use a road map like this? (the narrow strip). This map could show you where you are—if you happened to be at one of the places shown on the narrow strip. But a map is not only to show you where you are, but also where you have been and where you are going.

On the evening of the first Easter two of Jesus' followers felt like they were using a map like this. They were walking to Emmaus. They knew the way, so they didn't need a map. But they were confused by what had happened in the last three days. They knew Jesus was killed on the cross. Then some of the women who also followed Jesus said that His body was gone and an angel had said He was alive again. They couldn't understand what had happened.

As they walked along, Jesus joined them, but they didn't know who He was. They told Him why they felt lost and confused, and He said, "How foolish you are, how slow you are to believe everything the prophets said!"

The two men had thought only about the events of the last three days. That's like having a map only one inch wide. They only knew where they were at that time. Then Jesus, starting with the first books of the Bible, explained how God had said that the Messiah would suffer, die, and come back to life. That's like looking on a road map to see where you have been. (Open the map and place the strip in its proper place.) See, now the map makes more sense. It shows where you are (point to a spot on the center of the strip), but it also shows where you have been (point to area to left or below the place previously indicated).

When the disciples recognized Jesus, they were no longer confused. They understood what had happened on Good Friday and Easter because they remembered that God had told about the Messiah who would die for the sins of the world.

At times we also get confused about things that happen. We sometimes feel that the only map for our lives is a narrow strip that shows only where we are at the moment.

But remember, God gives a complete map of our life. He shows us where we have been, where we are, and also where we are going (point to area to right or above the place on the strip). Christ's death and resurrection is a part of your past. When you believe that, Jesus also becomes a part of your present and your future.

Know His Voice

The Word

Jesus said, "The man who goes in by the door is the shepherd of the sheep. The gatekeeper opens the gate for him; the sheep hear his voice as he calls his own sheep by name, and he leads them out. When he has brought them out, he goes ahead of them, and the sheep follow him, because they know his voice. They will not follow someone else; instead, they will run away from him, because they do not know his voice." John 10:2-5 (From the Gospel for the Fourth Sunday of Easter)

The World

Prior to the worship service, use a cassette recorder to record voices of parents of children who will attend. Ask the parent to say the name of the child and add a personal phrase (not a command) such as: "I've got a surprise for you." "Happy birthday." "I like having you around."

I have several messages recorded on this cassette player. I'm going to play it for all of you to hear. Since all of you will hear the same words from the same tape, you should receive the same message. But I think some of you will hear something different than the others. Let's see.

(Play the cassette messages.)

You all heard the same words. But the message was different for some of you. It was different, first of all, because your name was called. When you hear your name, you listen more carefully. But other people have the same name you heard on the tape. Yet those who heard their name on the cassette knew that the message was for them. The message was for them because they also recognized the voice of the person who called, their name and spoke the message. The message meant more to those children who recognized their parent's voice because they knew the person who was speaking.

Jesus tells us that we must also learn to recognize His voice and to know that He calls us by our name. He says He is like a shepherd who calls his own sheep by name and leads them to the pasture. The sheep would not follow another shepherd because they would not recognize his voice.

If Jesus is to be your Shepherd and you are to follow Him, you must hear Him call your name and you must recognize His voice.

Jesus called you by your name when you were baptized in His name. When you believe that God created you and hears your prayers, you know that He knows you as an individual and cares about you. When you know that Christ died for you and paid for your sins, you know that He knows you. When you see Him raised from the dead and know that He has invited you to heaven, you know He is calling you by name.

Not only does Jesus call your name, but you also can recognize His voice. His voice gives you comfort and peace. His voice tells you of love. His voice makes you patient and understanding.

Jesus calls you by name and tells you that He loves you.

The One Way That Works

The Word

Jesus answered him, "I am the Way, the Truth, and the Life; no one goes to the Father except by Me." John 14:6 (From the Gospel for the Fifth Sunday of Easter)

The World

A lock and key with an assortment of extra keys.

Jesus said He is the Way—the way to heaven. He did not just show us the way to heaven by telling us what to do, but He is the way to heaven because He paid for our sins and opened the door to eternal life.

Jesus said He is the Truth—truth that we can believe in. He not only told us the truth, but He is the Truth. He is holy and perfect, so He could be the sacrifice for us.

Jesus said He is the Life—life that He shares with us. Jesus not only lives for us, but He gave His own life in our place. Because He rose from the dead we can be a part of His new life.

We like to know that Jesus is the Way, the Truth and the Life. But listen to what else He said. He added, "No one goes to the Father except by Me." Jesus is the only Way, the only Truth and the only Life.

Since we know God loves all people and wants all people to be in heaven, we sometimes want to avoid the part of the message from Jesus that says He is the only way to be saved. But we need not hide His words. When Jesus tells us no one can be saved except by Him, He is showing us that all people can be saved by Him because He is the Way, the Truth and the Life for all people.

Look at it this way. See this lock. Suppose it locked the door to heaven. You need a key to open the lock. Here is one (wrong key). But it won't open the lock. This key won't either. Nor this one. None of these keys fit the lock. But look at this key (the right one). See, it opens the lock. This key opens the lock because its ridges and bumps match the ridges and bumps in the lock.

You might say that you'd rather use one of the other keys. Maybe one of them is prettier, easier to find, or cheaper. But if they won't open the lock they are of no help to you.

Sin is the lock that keeps us out of heaven. Jesus is the only key that opens the lock of sin. Only because He is perfect, yet willing to die for us, can He be our Savior. The fact that Jesus is both God and human, that He died and rose again, those things are the ridges and bumps that allow Him to open the lock of sin so we can be with God.

We can talk about other ways to go to heaven. But the other ways can't remove the problem of sin. Jesus has. He is the Way, the Truth, and the Life. And through Him all people can be saved.

One Helper After Another

The Word

Jesus said, "I will ask the Father, and He will give you another Helper, the Spirit of truth, to stay with you forever. The world cannot receive Him, because it cannot see Him or know Him. But you know Him, because He remains with you and lives in you." John 14:16-17 (From the Gospel for the Sixth Sunday of Easter)

The World

Two kinds of medicine.

Suppose you had a very bad cold. You were so sick you had to go to a doctor. The doctor might give you medicine like this (first bottle) to make you well. Then he might give you some more medicine like this (second) for you to take to keep you in good health. The first medicine was to cure you. The second included vitamins to keep you from getting sick again.

In our Bible reading Jesus tells us that God also has two kinds of help for us. Jesus is our first helper. He came to cure our sickness of sin. Just as medicine fights the germs in our body, Jesus fought against the sin that is in us. He had to die in our place in order to destroy sin's power to kill us. But He won the battle, because He came back to life. He is the nelper who cured our sin.

But then listen to what He said, "I will ask the Father, and He will give you another Helper, the Spirit of truth, to stay with you forever." Not only has God given us the first helper, Jesus, to cure our sin, but He also gives us another helper, the Holy Spirit, who will stay with us forever and help prevent sin in our lives.

Jesus has already paid for all of our guilt, and now the Holy Spirit continues to come to us to help us fight against temptation and sin. The Holy Spirit helps us live as Christian people; so we can enjoy the new life that Jesus has given to us as we help one another.

God's second helper, the Holy Spirit, works with us today each time we hear the message of Jesus' love for us. The Holy Spirit brings us to faith in Jesus and keeps the faith alive so we know that God is always with us.

Jesus also tells us, "The world cannot receive Him [that is, the Holy Spirit, the second helper], because it cannot see Him or know Him. But you know Him, because He remains with you and lives in you."

No one can start with the second helper. A person cannot take the medicine that prevents the sickness until he has taken the medicine that cures the sickness. First each person needs to know Jesus Chirst as his Savior from sin. Then he can also know the Holy Spirit as a helper who keeps the love and forgiveness of Christ in his daily life.

From Heaven to Earth to Heaven

The Word

Jesus said, "I showed Your glory on earth; I finished the work You gave me to do. Father! Give Me glory in Your presence now, the same glory I had with You before the world was made." John 17:4-5 (From the Gospel for the Seventh Sunday of Easter)

The World

A lighted candle, if possible one used regularly in worship, such as an Eternal Light or altar candle.

This candle is on our altar for a special purpose. We don't use it to make light. We have other lights to use when the church is dark. This candle is to remind us that Jesus is the Light of the world. When you see the candle, you remember that Jesus shows you the way to heaven.

But suppose I came into the church at night when the electricity was off and I wanted to find a book. Without electricity the other lights would not help me. But I could take this candle from the altar and use it for light. After I found the book, I could put the candle back on the altar. The candle would again be a reminder of Christ, but for a while it had served a practical purpose to make light so I could find something.

This candle is like Jesus in another way. He had a special, honored place in heaven. In our Bible reading He says, "Father! Give Me glory in Your presence now, the same glory I had with You before the world was made." Before He came to earth, Jesus lived in the glory of heaven, a place of honor like the candle on the altar.

Then we needed Him on earth. He had to come here to find us, to take away our sin, to show us the way back to the Father.

That is like taking the candle from the altar and using it to search for something. Jesus made Himself useful for all people when He came to die in our place. In our Bible reading He says, "I showed Your glory on earth; I finished the work You gave Me to do."

After Jesus finished His work on earth, He ascended back to heaven. Just as I put the candle back on the altar where it had been before, Jesus returned to the glory of heaven where He had been before.

When we worship Jesus today, we think of Him as being in heaven. He shares in the glory of God. He has prepared a place with Him for us. We know that someday we can go to be with Him; because we know that He first came to be with us.

Watch Who Is Breathing on You

The Word

Then Jesus said to them again, "Peace be with you. As the Father sent Me, so I send you." He said this, and then He breathed on them and said, "Receive the Holy Spirit. If you forgive men's sins, they are forgiven; if you do not forgive them, they are not forgiven." John 20:21-23 (From the Gospel for the Day of Pentecost)

The World

Your breath and the breath of others.

Hold your hand over your nose and mouth and breathe. Feel your breath? Except on a chilly morning, you can never see your breath. Since the air you breathe in and out is invisible, you never think about it unless, like now, someone reminds you. Or maybe you think about it when you have a cold and your mother tells you not to breathe on anyone because your breath carries the germs from your sickness. If you breathed on someone else, they might get your illness.

But listen to our Bible reading for today: "Jesus said this, and then He breathed on them and said, 'Receive the Holy Spirit.'"

When Jesus breathed on His disciples, they didn't catch a cold. They caught the Holy Spirit. We don't know exactly how Jesus breathed on those disciples. He probably didn't just blow in their faces. But He did give them something. Our Bible reading names the things the disciples received when Jesus breathed the Holy Spirit on them. They received peace and they received power to forgive sins.

And the disciples received the power to breath that same Spirit on others. Because they had received peace from Christ, the Holy Spirit gave them the power to bring peace to others.

Because Christ had forgiven their sins, they could tell others about His payment for all sins and share that forgiveness with others.

On this Pentecost Day you should ask yourself two questions:

First: Who is breathing on you? Some people share the love of Christ. They share peace, joy, understanding. When you share in the lives of people who live in Christ, you receive the blessings that they have.

Others will breathe anger, jealousy, hatred, lust, greed, and other hurtful feelings on you. Learn to recognize the bad feelings and do not let them become a part of your life.

Second: Who are you breathing on? Do you share the peace you have? Do you forgive others when you know you are forgiven? What spirit are you breathing on others? Is it the Holy Spirit? The Spirit that shares the new life in Christ? That's the Spirit you receive. Pass it on.

What's in a Name?

The Word

Jesus said, "Go, then, to all peoples everywhere and make them My disciples: baptize them in the name of the Father, the Son, and the Holy Spirit." Matthew 28:19 (From the Gospel for the First Sunday After Pentecost)

The World

Two invitations in envelopes. Each reads: "You are invited to the White House Tuesday at 2 p. m." One is signed "Grandmother," the other with the name of the President of the United States.

Suppose your family, including your grandmother, went on vacation to Washington, D. C. While there, your grandmother leaves this invitation on your bed. (Read it.) Your grandmother has invited you on a tour of the White House where the President of the United States and his family live. Most tourists visit the White House when they are in the Capital City.

But suppose you visit the Senator from your home state and he gives you this. (Read the second invitation.) This invitation is the same, but it is signed by the President himself. The first invitation was for you to be a tourist and visit the White House. The second is for you to be a guest at the White House. Even though each invitation has the same words, the invitations are different because of the name of the person who sent it.

Think of the two invitations as you hear the Bible reading for today. Jesus says, "Go, then, to all peoples everywhere and make them My disciples: baptize them in the name of the Father, the Son, and the Holy Spirit."

You have been invited to see Jesus as your Savior and to be baptized. Most of you have accepted the invitation. But the person who invited you to be with Jesus did not invite you as a tourist. The invitation was not like the one from your grandmother. Instead you were invited as a guest, because the invitation was given in the name of the Father and the Son and the Holy Spirit. Just as the President might give invitations to the White House through Senators, and yet they are given in the President's name; so also God gives invitations through people, but the invitation is given in God's name.

You accept the invitation as a guest, not as a tourist, because you are invited, not just to see God, but to be with Him. When your invitation comes in the name of God the Father, you know that God remembers He has created you and that He wants you to be with Him. The invitation in the name of God the Son says Jesus has died for you and has given you eternal life in His name. The invitation from God the Holy Spirit tells you that the Spirit will continue to come to you to help your faith grow.

You receive many invitations to be with God. The invitations come through many people—all of those who tell you the great things God is doing for you. But each invitation comes in the name of the Father, the Son, and the Holy Spirit. God wants you to be with Him.

After Hearing Comes Doing

The Word

Jesus said, "So then, everyone who hears these words of Mine and obeys them will be like a wise man who built his house on the rock. . . . But everyone who hears these words of Mine and does not obey them will be like a foolish man who built his house on the sand." Matthew 7:24, 26 (From the Gospel for the Second Sunday After Pentecost)

The World

Two figures of children cut from paper, four Band-Aids, a large rock or brick, a box of sand (kitty litter will do).

We all know we should hear the Word of God. But when we hear what Jesus tells us in today's Bible reading, we also find out that we need to do more than hear the Word. We also must do what the Word says.

First let's think about hearing the Word of God. These two children (the paper figures) will represent all of us, and these Band-Aids will represent the Word of God. The children hear the Word. (Place a Band-Aid on each ear of each figure.) See— they hear the Word of God. It has become a part of them.

Jesus says if we hear His words and do what He says, we are like a wise person who builds his house on a rock. When we hear God's Word, we remember that the words come from God. So just as they are a part of us when we hear them, the words are a part of God because He spoke them. (Use the tapes to fasten one of the figures to the rock.)

When we hear God's Word that tells us we are sinners, we can do His Word by repenting and asking for His help. We are then fastened to God by His Word. When we hear God's Word that tells us we are forgiven by Jesus and that He always loves and helps us, we are fastened to God by Jesus' love and we do

His Word by loving God and by loving other people. Then God's Word holds us close to Him like the wise man who built his house on a rock.

But if we hear God's Word and do not do it, we are like a person who builds his house on the sand. See, this person (the second figure) also heard the Word. But when this person heard that we are sinners, he did not repent and ask for God's help; nor did he receive forgiveness from that Word that tells us of Jesus' taking our sins on Himself. The words came to his ears; but he was not attached to God by Jesus' love, and he did not do the words by loving God and other people. (Place the figure in the sand.) See— I cannot tape the figure to the sand. The person is not fastened to anything if he only hears the Word but does not do it. He is fastened only to the sand and can easily be moved. But the first is fastened to the rock and receives God's power through the Word.

You hear God's Word each time you read the Bible, study about God's Word, or come to church. Each time you hear the Word, look for ways to do it. When you both hear and do the Word, you are fastened to God by the love that Jesus gives to you.

Why Aren't You with the Sinners?

The Word

Some Pharisees saw this and said to His disciples, "Why does your teacher eat with tax collectors and outcasts?" Jesus heard them and answered, "People who are well do not need a doctor, but only those who are sick." Matthew 9:11-12 (From the Gospel for the Third Sunday After Pentecost)

The World

Two radios—one of them in nonworking condition (remove batteries if necessary). A large poster that says "Radio Sales" on one side and "Perfect People" on the other. Another poster with "Radio Repair" on one side and "People Who Need Help" on the other.

I'm going to set up a radio shop here. First I have a place to sell radios (put up first sign). Here I have a good radio. (Turn it on to show that it works.) But our shop also has a place to repair radios. (Put up the second sign.) See, this radio does not work.

Now if I asked you to work in my radio shop, which department would you want to work in? Would you rather sell the radio that works, or repair the one that does not work? Unless you have been trained to fix radios, you had better try to sell. Few of us could repair a radio, but most of us could sell one. Only a specially trained person can do the repair work.

Now let's make our store into a people show. (Turn both signs over.) This part (first sign) would be for the perfect people. And this part (second sign) would be for people who need help. Where would you be in this shop? Are you like the radio that works? Or the one that needs repair?

Since we are alive, we are all in operating condition. We can talk, walk, play, work, and think. But we are not in perfect operating condition. God made us to be perfect. Each time we say bad things, or cheat, or steal, or hurt ourselves or someone else, we need to be repaired. Each time we fail to help others who need our help, we show that we are not working like we should. Though we would like to be in the part of the store for the perfect people, and sometimes we pretend we belong there, we all need to be in the repair department.

Jesus also came to be in the repair department of the people shop. Some people complained because Jesus always spent His time with people who admitted they were sinners. He ate dinner with people who had bad reputations. Others, who pretended they were good, asked His disciples, "Why does your teacher eat with tax collectors and outcasts?"

Jesus heard the question and answered, "People who are well do not need a doctor, but only those who are sick." He tells us that He came to earth because we are sinners. And He came to make us well again. Only Jesus could take the job of forgiving sinners, because He is the only human who is also God and the only One who could give His life for us. Because He was perfect, He could make us perfect by giving His life for us.

Because we know Jesus has forgiven us, we can share His love with all people. People asked Jesus' disciples why He spent His time with sinners. Should we ask each other, "Why aren't we spending more time with sinners?" We know the way to help them because we know Jesus, who is the Savior of all.

Know When to Ask for Help

The Word

So He [Jesus] said to His disciples, "There is a large harvest, but few workers to gather it in. Pray to the Owner of the harvest that He will send out workers to gather in His harvest." Matthew 9:37-38 (From the Gospel for the Fourth Sunday After Pentecost)

The World

A large box of breakfast cereal, six cereal bowls, six spoons.

When Jesus walked through the towns where He lived, He saw many people. He healed some people, answered questions for others, and one time He preached a sermon to 5,000 people.

But Jesus did not have time to talk to all the people. Many would not come to hear Him. Others listened for a while, then left Him. As He saw the big crowds of people, He was sad. He said, "There is a large harvest, but few workers to gather it in. Pray to the Owner of the harvest that He will send out workers to gather in His harvest."

Jesus said that the crowds of people were like a crop in a field ready to be harvested. He had good news for them—good news that He would give them eternal life. But He had only a few disciples to help tell all the people. He knew He needed more help.

We can understand the problem Jesus had this way: Suppose you had to fix breakfast for six people. Here is a box of cereal. It has enough food for six people. And here are six bowls. Pour the cereal into the bowls and you're ready. But look, I have only one spoon. There's plenty of food, but only one spoon. Each person would have to take a bite and pass the spoon around. Or else they would have to take turns eating. Of course, we can find a better solution. Get more spoons. Here are five more spoons; so everyone can eat.

The good news that Jesus loves all people and died for all is like this big box of cereal. God has enough love for everyone. And all people need it. But more people are needed to share the good news. When only a few Christians tell others about the love of Jesus, they are like the breakfast with one spoon. Many people will have to wait to receive the love that Christ has for them.

But instead of making people wait to learn more about Jesus, let's do what Jesus said. He told us to pray for more workers. Let's pray right now:

Dear Lord Jesus, thank You for sending workers to tell us about Your life for us. We are glad that we know You are our Savior. Continue to bless those who told us, so they can tell many more people about Your love.

We also ask You to send more workers to our community and to the world to share the message of Your love. Use each of us to be workers in our homes, neighborhoods, and schools. Help us to show Your love in our lives and to speak about You with our voices.

We also pray for those who are Your workers in other countries. Let Your Holy Spirit bless their work; and open our hearts to help support those who work for You. Amen.

Wear Your Hat

The Word

Jesus said: "Whoever declares publicly that he belongs to Me, I will do the same for him before My Father in heaven. But whoever denies publicly that he belongs to Me, then I will deny him before My Father in heaven." Matthew 10:32-33 (From the Gospel for the Fifth Sunday After Pentecost)

The World

A hat similar to one worn by an attendant at an amusement park (make one by printing "Six Flags" on a plain hat). Another hat with a large cross on it.

Today I'm going to be the manager of an amusement park, and I will hire each of you as attendants. Your job is to pick up the litter in the park and to help the other employees. This hat will show that you work for me. Since I don't have a hat for everyone, I'll ask Dave to come up and represent each of you. David, you wear the hat. As long as you are wearing it, you can go on any ride or see any show in the park. Isn't that great!

But when you're wearing the hat, you must also do anything that the guests and other employees ask. You may have to clean up a spilled ice cream cone, find a lost baby, help a child who fell in a lake. If people keep asking you to work, you might want to take the hat off. (Do it.) Now no one will know you work for me, so you won't have to work. But now you can't ride the rides or see the shows. You have to decide, do you want to wear the hat or not?

Jesus gives us the same kind of choice when He says, "Whoever declares publicly that he belongs to Me, I will do the same for him before My Father in heaven. But whoever denies publicly that he belong to Me, then I will deny him before My Father in heaven."

When we become Christians we put a hat on. (Put the second hat on the child.) The hat is invisible, but we'll use this hat with a cross to show how it works. The hat means you believe in Christ. The cross shows that Jesus died for you and you belong to Him. When you wear the hat, you are telling everyone that Christ is your Savior.

As long as you have the hat on, God is with you. He will hear your prayers. He will forgive your sins. He will take you to heaven.

But when you wear the hat, people will ask you to live like a Christian. You will be asked to help hungry people. You will be asked to love people you don't even like. You will be asked to forgive those who have hurt you. You will be asked to tell others what Jesus has done for them.

If people keep asking you to do the things Jesus told you to do, you may want to take the hat off. But remember Jesus said, "Whoever denies publicly that he belongs to Me, then I will deny him before My Father in heaven."

Of course, we Christians don't have a hat like this. This hat is only a reminder. Ask yourself: Do others know I am a Christian? Do they ask me to help them because they know I love Jesus and Jesus loves them? Do I hide my faith from others so I do not have to help them?

As you answer such questions, remember Jesus' promise, "Whoever declares publicly that he belongs to Me, I will do the same for him before My Father in heaven."

Wear your hat.

Are You Lost? Or Found?

The Word

Jesus said, "Whoever tries to gain his own life will lose it; whoever loses his life for My sake will gain it." Matthew 10:39 (From the Gospel for the Sixth Sunday After Pentecost.)

The World

A box labeled "Lost and Found" containing a variety of items including a child's watch.

Lost is the opposite of found. Right? See this watch. If I lost it (drop it) I would not have a watch. Then when I found it, I would have it back again.

But now the watch is in a box called "Lost and Found." Is the watch lost? Or is it found? The watch is lost and found at the same time. The person who owns the watch does not know where it is. For that person it is lost. But someone else found the watch and put it in this box. For that person, it is found. Anything in this box is lost from its owner's point of view, but it has been found by someone else.

Jesus tells us that we can be in a "Lost and Found" box. Listen to the Bible reading for today, "Whoever tries to gain his own life will lose it; whoever loses his life for My sake will gain it."

Jesus says we can lose our lives. We can lose our lives by not going to heaven. We can also lose our lives by losing our purpose for living. If we waste our lives by not doing what we can do, by not enjoying our own life, and by not helping others; then we lose our lives.

If we try to find ourselves, we will always be lost. If you were lost in the woods and were found by someone who was also lost, you would still be lost. You cannot find your own life by trying to save yourself for eternal life or by making your own life worthwhile.

But when we know we are lost, we find out what it means that Jesus is our Savior. He finds us. He came looking for us. His search for us included death itself, because He knew all of us must die. He found us and offers us a new life, because He came back from the grave.

You and I are like this watch. By ourselves we would be lost. We do not always serve the purpose for which God created us. But Jesus has found us. He has put us in the "Lost and Found" box. He tells us that as long as we are with Him, we are found. As long as we are with Him, we know the way back to heaven. As long as we are with Him, we can live a life on earth that has purpose and meaning.

You were lost. But you have been found!

Take the Right Load

The Word

Jesus said, "Come to Me, all of you who are tired from carrying your heavy loads, and I will give you rest. Take My yoke and put it on you, and learn from Me, because I am gentle and humble in spirit; and you will find rest. The yoke I will give you is easy, and the load I will put on you light." Matthew 11:28-30 (From the Gospel for the Seventh Sunday After Pentecost)

The World

Two boxes loaded with bricks or other heavy items. Tape.

How much do you think one of these boxes weighs? The boxes weigh very little. But what's in them is heavy. See. (Lift each box.) If you had a job to carry boxes like this all day, you'd be worn out by night.

Or even worse, what if you had to carry a load like this all this time. From your bed to the bathroom to brush your teeth, to the table to eat, down the steps to go outside. Carrying this load would wear you out.

In some ways our sins are like the weight in this box. When we carry guilty feelings around with us, we can't enjoy life. They keep us from doing the good things we want to do. When we have done something wrong, we don't like ourselves and are afraid that others won't like us either. Being guilty is a heavy load.

But Jesus says something to us. He says, "Come to Me, all of you who are tired from carrying your heavy loads, and I will give you rest." Jesus invites us to come to Him. He takes the weight out of the box. (Do it.) Because He died to pay for our sins, He has removed the heavy load of guilt.

Now the box is light. Jesus took away the guilt but not the

box. We still carry it. But listen to what He says, "Take My yoke and put it on you, and learn from Me, because I am gentle and humble in spirit; and you will find rest. The yoke I will give you is easy, and the load I will put on you is light."

Jesus still gives us a load to carry, but He takes the weight of the guilt from the load. We still have a life to live. This box without the weight may look much like the other one, but it feels different. (Lift the two boxes.) Let's mark the empty box with a cross (make a cross on the box with tape) to show that it is different.

When you carry this load that Jesus gives you, you are reminded that He has made the load light. Then you remember to thank Him for being your Savior and you fight against sin; so the box is not filled again. Your empty box is also a reminder that you can help others. You can help remove their heavy load of guilt by taking them to hear Jesus say, "Come to Me, all of you who are tired from carrying your heavy loads, and I will give you rest."

Look at the two boxes. One has the heavy load of guilt. The other is light and easy. It is the chance to help yourself and others. Take the right load.

Let the Word Go Deep

The Word

Jesus said, "The seed that fell on rocky ground stands for those who receive the message gladly as soon as they hear it. But it does not sink deep in them, and they don't last long. So when trouble or persecution comes because of the message, they give up at once." Matthew 13:20-21 (From the Gospel for the Eighth Sunday After Pentecost)

The World

A block of wood, a hammer, and a large nail.

Jesus said that some people hear the message that He loves them and believe it for a while, but when they have a problem, they forget to use the love He has given them. He says they are like a plant that sprouts and grows but does not have deep roots.

We can't show how a plant grows now, but this block of wood and nail can show us the same thing. We are like the piece of wood. And the nail is the Word of God—the message that Jesus is our Savior. When we hear the Word, Jesus comes into our lives. He is a part of us. (Drive the nail lightly into the wood.) See how the nail becomes part of the wood. I can lift the wood by touching only the nail. The Word of God that tells us Christ is our Savior is God's way of lifting us out of sin into eternal life.

But Jesus tells us to let the Word go all the way into our lives. If the Word stays like a plant with only small roots, it can easily be pulled out. If I wiggle this nail a little, I can easily pull it out. (Do it.) Problems in life can make us forget the Word that God has given to help us. Think of some of the things that might make you forget God's message of love for you: when you are with people who you think would rather do wrong things than right; when you are sick or worried and think God is not helping you the way you want Him to; when you have done something wrong and are afraid that God won't love you anymore; when you do not read the Bible or hear His Word. When problems like these and others come to you, they will try to pull God's Word out of your life like I pulled the nail from the wood.

That's why Jesus tells us that His Word must grow deep in our lives. You need to know how much God loves you so when problems come, you know that God is still with you and that He will help you. (Drive the nail deeply into the wood.) When you hear that God forgives your sins, apply the message to all parts of your life. Remember how Jesus lived for you and that all of His life applies to all of your life.

When you do have problems, remember Jesus' promise to be with you always. Know that no problem, not even death, can take the love of God from you because Christ has won every victory for you—He arose from the dead. When you know how God's love in Christ applies to all parts of your life and at all times, His Word is deep into your life. It cannot be pulled out. He has a way to hold on to you forever.

Our Job Is Not to Throw Away

The Word

"Do you want us to go and pull up the weeds?" they asked Him. "No," He answered, "because as you gather the weeds, you might pull up some of the wheat along with them. Let the wheat and the weeds both grow together until harvest, and then I will tell the harvest workers: Pull up the weeds first and tie them in bundles to throw in the fire; then gather in the wheat and put it in my barn." Matthew 13:28b-30 (From the Gospel for the Ninth Sunday After Pentecost)

The World

A composition book that is stapled or stiched together so if one page is torn out another will fall out. You can make your own by folding paper and stapling at the fold.

Jesus told a story to teach us that we are not to get rid of people who do evil things. In His story a farmer had both wheat and weeds in the same field. The servants wanted to pull out the weeds. But the farmer said that they would also pull out wheat and destroy the crops. He told the servants to wait until harvesttime, when the weeds would be separated from the wheat.

We could compare His story to this: If you were writing an assignment for school in this book and made a mistake, you might want to tear out the page. But if you did (do it), you would not only tear out the page with the mistake, but another page would also come out. So when you tore out the bad page, you would also lose a good page.

Sometimes we think that bad people should be destroyed— like tearing out a page with a mistake. Some people cause wars, commit crimes, destroy property, and do other evil things. They are a messed-up page. We want to tear them out and throw them away.

But God tells us that we cannot decide who should be thrown away. If we think we have the right to punish those who are wrong, we will also hurt poeple whose sins are forgiven by Jesus or those who will be forgiven when they learn about Him.

God tells us that those who do evil will be punished. When the world ends, He will send His angels to separate the good from the bad. But the angels are to do that job. Not us.

Our job is to be a good page in the book. All of us have done wrong things. But God did not tear us out and throw us away. Instead, He sent Jesus to be our Savior. Jesus cleaned up our lives. He lets us stay with God. He promises us that on the final Judgment Day He will take us with Him to heaven.

While we are here, we cannot let the wrongs of others take us away from God. We cannot excuse our sins by saying that others did it first. Instead, we are to let others see that we are forgiven so they also can know that Jesus loves them and they also can be saved.

What Comes First in Your Life?

The Word

Jesus said, "Also, the kingdom of heaven is like a buyer looking for fine pearls. When he finds one that is unusually fine, he goes and sells everything he has, and buys the pearl." Matthew 13:45-46 (From the Gospel for the Tenth Sunday After Pentecost)

The Word

That evening His [Jesus'] disciples came to Him and said, "It is already very late, and this is a lonely place. Send the people away and let them go to the villages and buy food for themselves." "They don't have to leave," answered Jesus. "You yourselves give them something to eat." "All we have here are five loaves and two fish," they replied. . . . He broke the loaves and gave them to the disciples, and the disciples gave them to the people. Everyone ate and had enough. Matthew 14:15-17, 19b-20a (From the Gospel for the Eleventh Sunday After Pentecost)

Jesus told a story about a pearl buyer who found a special pearl; so he sold all his other pearls and bought the one perfect gem. You probably don't collect pearls, or know anyone who does, but you could understand Jesus' story this way:

The kingdom of heaven is like a boy who went fishing. He caught several nice fish (show the smaller fish) and thought he had a good catch. Then he caught one big fish. (Show the big fish.) So he threw all the small fish back in the lake and ran home to show everyone the one big fish.

That may be a fun story, but don't forget that it started by saying, "The kingdom of heaven is like . . . " That story is like our being in the kingdom of heaven, because we, like the boy with the five fish, have many nice things happen to us.

This fish (show the small fish again) is like the new bicycle you have. This one is for your home and family. This is your good grades or your place on a ball team or in a music group.

You can think of many other good things that have happened to you. All of those good things make us happy. We like to talk about them.

But something much greater has happened to us. God has sent His Son to be our Savior. God loves us so much that He asked Jesus to live with us, to show us a new way to live, and to make it possible for us to live His new way by giving us His Holy Spirit with power for the new life.

Because Jesus is our Savior, we can enjoy our life on earth. Even when we have pain and sorrow, we know He is with us. We can forgive others because we are forgiven. We can help others because He has helped us. Even when we die, we know He will raise us from the dead and we will live with Him forever.

Our faith in Jesus is like the one big fish. It makes us forget the other blessings in life. Knowing Jesus becomes the most important part of our life. We want to tell others about Him. We want to tell what He has done for us.

The other gifts in our lives are good gifts. They also come from God. But the gift of Jesus Christ is the one great gift. Knowing Him as our Savior is the gift that will last forever.

The More You Give,
the More You Can Give

The World

Five fish, 5 to 8 inches long, cut out of paper, and one fish 2 feet long.

The World

A box of cookies.

Wes, I need your help. Here is a cookie. (Don't show the box.) It's snack time and you have a cookie to eat. But look at all of the other kids here. (If possible include all children present—you'll need a cookie for each. Otherwise, invite 10 to the front to participate.) Would you eat your cookie in front of them when they have nothing to eat? I hope not.

One time Jesus' disciples had food for themselves but none for the five thousand people who had come to hear Jesus. They asked Jesus to send the people away to buy their own food. But Jesus told the disciples to divide their food with the crowd.

If I told you to divide your cookie with all the kids here, you'd say the cookie isn't big enough. And that's what the disciples told Jesus about their lunch. But Jesus had an answer. He asked the disciples to give their food to Him. He blessed it and gave it back. The disciples gave the food to the crowd, and everyone had enough to eat. They even had leftovers.

Let's try it. You give the cookie to me. We pray, "Thank you, God, that we have one cookie and that we have friends with whom we can share. Amen."

Now, Wes, give cookies to your friends. (Give him the box to pass around.) You know where the extra cookies came from, don't you? I had them hidden. I gave them to you. But remember, I gave you the first cookie too. And you were willing to give it back to me. Now you have not only the one cookie but also enough to share.

We know it is a miracle that Jesus could feed five thousand people with five loaves of bread and two fish. But remember that the five loaves and two fish were also from God. They also were miracles, gifts of God's love. God gave the disciples food for themselves. When they were willing to give it back to Jesus, He gave them much more.

Jesus did the same with His own life. God gave Jesus to people on earth. Then Jesus gave Himself to pay for our sins, when He died on the cross. But God raised Him from the dead and gave Him back to us.

When God tells us to give to others, we are sometimes afraid to give away what we have. But if we see ourselves giving back to God what He has given to us, we remember that what we have, first came from God. And God always has more to give.

A Faith to Hold On To

The Word

Then Peter spoke up. "Lord," he said, "if it is really You, order me to come out on the water to You." "Come!" answered Jesus. So Peter got out of the boat and started walking on the water to Jesus. When he noticed the wind, however, he was afraid and started to sink down in the water. "Save me, Lord!" he cried. At once Jesus reached out and grabbed him and said, "How little faith you have! Why did you doubt?" Matthew 14:27-31 (From the Gospel for the Twelfth Sunday After Pentecost)

The World

A basketball and a rope.

I've asked Sue to help me as we talk about our Bible reading for today. First, Sue, I want you to hold on to this rope. Hold on tight with both hands, as though you were climbing a mountain and needed the rope to keep from falling. That's fine.

Now, catch the ball! (Throw the ball to the child without notice. Discuss briefly the child's reaction according to her decision. Why did she drop the rope to catch the ball? Or why did she miss the ball to hold on to the rope?) Thank you, Sue.

In our Bible reading Peter also had to make a choice. He saw Jesus walking on the water, and he knew that Jesus could do such an amazing thing because He was God as well as man. He also knew that Jesus offered to share His power with those who believed. So Peter asked Jesus for the power to walk on water. And Jesus gave it to him. Peter's faith was like this rope. The faith connected Peter to Jesus, and as long as Peter held on to it, he could walk on water.

Then Peter saw the wind. He felt the water on the bottom of his feet in a way he had never felt before. He remembered that people don't walk on water. He forgot the power that came to

Him through Jesus and remembered only what life was like without Jesus. He let lose of the power of Jesus and reached for his own power. Then he started to sink. Jesus reached out and pulled him back up and towed him back to the boat.

You and I also face the same kind of choices in our lives. We know Jesus is our Savior. He has reached out to us, to love us, to pay for our sins, to give us a new life. He offers to give us all of His power when we believe in Him. We hold on to Jesus by our faith in Him.

But we also are tempted to drop the rope of faith. Our faith tells us we are forgiven and that we can forgive others. But sometimes we want to drop our grip on faith so we can live in our own guilt or refuse to forgive someone else. Our faith tells us God loves us because He loves all people. Sometimes we want to drop the faith so we don't have to love someone else.

You look at your own life. First see how Jesus has thrown you a rope so He can share His power with you. Then see what else is being thrown at you—what other things make you want to leave go of your faith to grab something else.

A Faith That Is Great

The Word

So Jesus answered her, "You are a woman of great faith! What you want will be done for you." And at that very moment her daughter was healed. Matthew 15:28 (From the Gospel for the Thirteenth Sunday After Pentecost)

The World

A picture of Jesus with four hooks taped on it at various places. Four ribbons of different colors, each with a ring on one end.

In our Bible reading Jesus tells a woman she has a great faith. What would He say about our faith? Faith is difficult to measure. One's faith is not great because it is longer, heavier, older than another's. We need a special way to measure faith. Let's try to find one.

Here is a picture of Jesus. We are talking about faith in Him. The woman's faith was great because she believed in Him. But Jesus said that her faith was greater than others who believed in Him.

For example, we believe that Jesus can make us well when we are sick. I'll put this blue ribbon on Jesus to show that faith. Faith is like the ribbon. When I hold on to the faith, it connects me to Jesus, because I believe He will heal me. Our Bible reading is about a woman who believed that Jesus would heal her daughter.

We also believe Jesus will answer our prayers. This green ribbon will show that faith. I hook my faith in Jesus like this when I pray that He will help me get good grades, make friends, be a good ballplayer.

And I believe Jesus forgives my sins. I hook this red ribbon to Jesus to show how I hold on to my faith in Him because He forgives me. We could put many more ribbons on the picture to

97

show how we have faith in Jesus. But if your faith holds on to only one of these ribbons, you have a problem.

If you believe in Jesus only because He heals the sick (grab blue ribbon), what will happen if you get sick and are not healed? Some people are sick. Some never get well. At first Jesus did not heal the woman's daughter in our story. If she believed only when Jesus healed, her faith would have stopped. (Remove the blue ribbon.)

Or if you believe only when God says yes to your prayers (take green ribbon), you have a problem when He says no. God does say no sometimes. He said no to Job and to Paul. Does a no end your faith? (Take off green ribbon.) If you believe only when your sins are forgiven, what happens when you feel you have committed a sin greater than any before? Will it make you lose your faith? (Take off red ribbon.)

A faith that is great includes all of these (put ribbons back on) plus more. This white ribbon will show us that we have faith that Jesus is our Lord and Savior. (Put white ribbon on and hold all the ribbons together in one hand.) Jesus is Lord of our lives even when we don't understand why we have problems. He is Lord and Savior even when we hurt and are afraid. Our faith is great when we hold on to Him through any problem and through any joy. Our faith is great when nothing can separate us from Him.

What Do You Say About Jesus?

The Word

[Jesus] asked His disciples: "Who do men say the Son of Man is?" "Some say John the Baptist," they answered. "Others say Elijah, while others say Jeremiah or some other prophet." "What about you?" He asked them. "Who do you say I am?" Simon Peter answered, "You are the Messiah, the Son of the living God." Matthew 16:13b-16 (From the Gospel for the Fourteenth Sunday After Pentecost)

The World

A loaf of bread.

What is this (the bread)? The answer is easy. This is a loaf of bread. Of course, you could give other answers. You could say it is flour, water, butter, yeast, and other things that have been baked together. Or you could say this is stuff to make sandwiches with. Or something to toast. But right now, this is a loaf of bread.

Jesus once asked His disciples who people said He was. The disciples said that some people thought He was John the Baptist, who had come to prepare the way for the Savior. Others thought Jesus was one of many Old Testament prophets who had promised a Savior would come.

Then Jesus asked the disciples who they thought Jesus was. Peter answered for all of them when he said, "You are the Messiah, the Son of the living God." And Peter was right. The other answers had talked about a Savior who was coming. But Peter saw Jesus as the Savior who was there. He knew that Jesus was not just another man, but that He was God's Son, who had come to be a part of the human race. He knew Jesus was the sacrifice to pay for the sin of the world. And Jesus said Peter's answer was right.

What about you? Who do you say that Jesus is? We can talk about what used to be. Jesus was the one born in a stable of a virgin mother. He cured sick people and raised several dead people back to life. He died and rose again. All of that is true. But to speak of Jesus only in the past is like calling this (the bread) flour, shortening, and milk. Something has happened to the flour, shortening, and milk to make it become this. Something has also happened to the Savior who lived long ago.

Or we could say that Jesus is the One who will return to judge the earth. Then He will take us to heaven. This is also true. But this is the same as calling the bread stuff you can use to make a sandwich or toast. That will happen. But the bread is bread right now.

Jesus is our Lord and Savior today. Because we know what He has done and what He will do, we also know what He is right now. He is the Lord of our lives. He guides and leads us. He calls us to follow Him. He asks us to serve Him by serving other people. That's for today. He loves us now and accepts us now. He forgives us today.

Know What You Need

The Word

Jesus asked, "Will a man gain anything if he wins the whole world but loses his life? Of course not! There is nothing a man can give to regain his life." Matthew 16:26 (From the Gospel for the Fifteenth Sunday After Pentecost)

The World

A pet gerbil, hamster, or rabbit. (If not available, use a stuffed toy and ask the children to pretend.) A collection of accessories for the pet and some pet food.

Suppose this is your hamster. You might enjoy having a pet. But owning a pet means you also have to take care of it. Since you like your pet, you want it to have a nice home. So the pet needs good care. Then the pet needs this exerciser. Then the pet needs this toy. And it needs a waterer.

Since you are spending all your money on the pet, you would think that you are taking good care of it. Most pets don't have all these fancy things in their cages. Your pet is lucky.

But if you are spending all your allowance on trinkets for your hamster and not buying this (the food), your pet is not lucky. In fact, your pet will die. The other things may be nice for your pet to have, but the food is more than nice. It is necessary. The pet must have the food or it will die.

Now think about how God takes care of us. We are not God's pets. We are His children because He created us. His Son Jesus came to be our brother. But the way a child might take care of a pet can help us understand how God takes care of us.

God has many wonderful things to give us in life. We have homes, cars, schools, vacations, television, toys, clothes, food. We say we need those things and we do. But Jesus asks a question: "Will a man gain anything if he wins the whole world but loses his life?" And Jesus gives the answer: "Of course not!"

Even if we have all the food we can eat, the best place to live, and perfect health, we will not live forever. If you owned everything in the world, you would still die. The hamster needs food to live as your pet. But for us to live as children of God, we need more than food. We need a way to have eternal life.

And God gives us eternal life in Jesus Christ. More important than the food, clothing, and all the other things that we need from God is the need for a way to live again after we die. Jesus died for us. And He lives again. Know what you need. And know that Jesus gives it to you.

When You See Someone Else Sin

The Word

Jesus said, "If your brother sins against you, go to him and show him his fault. But do it privately, just between yourselves. If he listens to you, you have won your brother back." Matthew 18:15 (From the Gospel for the Sixteenth Sunday After Pentecost)

The World

A wide felt-tip marker and a damp, soapy cloth.

I have asked Julia to help me today as we talk about our Bible reading. In it Jesus says, "If your brother sins against you, go to him and show him his fault. But do it privately, just between yourselves. If he listens to you, you have won your brother back."

I am going to make a mark on Julia's forehead (do it) to stand for a fault that Jesus talks about. Having a dirty face isn't a sin, but we'll use the mark as something we can see and pretend it is a sin. (As you talk, hold the marker pencil concealed in your hand and wipe your forehead to make a mark on yourself.)

Now if I follow what Jesus says I cannot ignore the mark on Julia's forehead. I can't just say, "That's her business. If she likes to have a dirty face, it makes no difference to me." Jesus says I must tell her.

On the other hand I can't yell, "Hey, everyone look at Julia. She has a dirty face." Or I can't go around to whisper to all the others and tell them about her problems. If I did either of those things, I wouldn't be helping her.

Jesus says that I must tell her about her wrong in private. He had several good reasons why we should tell others their faults in secret. First of all, we should do it for our own sakes. When I said, "Hey, look at Julia's face," did some of you notice the mark on my forehead? When we talk about other people's sins, others will not only see the fault on the person we point at but they will also see our sins. None of us are perfect. When we talk about other people's faults we also remind people of our own faults.

The other reason we are to tell a person their faults in private is that our purpose is to help them—not embarrass them. We don't tell them their sin to hurt them or to make them feel bad. Instead, we tell them and offer to help take away the problem. Here, Julia, I have a damp cloth that will wipe the mark off your forehead. Since I don't have a mirror, will you also help me, so we can both have clean faces.

Of course a damp cloth won't wipe away sin, but Jesus will. When we tell someone that they have done something wrong, we also tell them that Jesus has died on the cross to forgive them. He wipes the guilt away. And as we share the message of love and forgiveness with others, we also receive the same message for our own lives.

Are You in Favor of Forgiveness?

The Word

And Jesus concluded, "That is how My Father in heaven will treat you if you do not forgive your brother, every one of you, from your heart." Matthew 18:35 (From the Gospel for the Seventeenth Sunday After Pentecost)

The World

Four cloth napkins, a plastic bag, a pan of water.

Are you in favor of forgiveness?

All of us like forgiveness when we are the one who is wrong. When we have done something we should not have done, we want others to forgive us. We are glad when our parents, friends, teachers, and God forgive us.

But do you like forgiveness when the other person is wrong? Are you willing to forgive your brother or sister, your classmates, your parents, your teachers, or anyone else who might have hurt you?

Jesus wants to forgive us. When He forgives, He does not just say, "I'll forget about your sin." Instead, He takes our sins on Himself. He has suffered for the wrong that we have done. When He gives us forgiveness, He also tells us that we can give the same forgiveness to others.

It works this way: Suppose this napkin is you. See, it is dry, and for this lesson we'll say that to be dry means you need forgiveness. Jesus is like this pan of water. He offers to remove the dryness. When the napkin goes in the water it is no longer dry. Your sins are gone. You are forgiven.

But now you meet someone who has done something to hurt you. (Hold up a dry napkin.) He needs forgiveness. You can share your forgiveness with that person. (Place the two napkins together and squeeze them.) See, you have shared your forgiveness. The other napkin is wet too. Jesus tells us that we can pass on the forgiveness He has given to us. Don't worry about running out of forgiveness. There's always more where it came from. (Put the first napkin back in the water.)

But sometimes we don't want to share our forgiveness. We hold it to ourselves. (Put the wet napkin in the plastic bag.) Now when the wet napkin touches another (do it), the other does not get wet. The forgiveness is not shared.

But Jesus tells us that if we do not forgive others from our heart, our Father in heaven will not forgive us. The same plastic bag that keeps one from sharing forgiveness with others also keeps one from receiving forgiveness. When we refuse to forgive, God does not forgive us. He makes us dry again. (Put a dry napkin in the plastic bag.) Now the napkin cannot get wet even when it is put back in the water. (Do it.)

See yourself receiving forgiveness today. Then think of others who need to receive forgiveness from you. Share what you have.

Look Who Made the Deal

The Word

"These men who were hired last worked only one hour," they said, "while we put up with a whole day's work in the hot sun—yet you paid them the same as you paid us!" "Listen, friend," the owner answered one of them, "I have not cheated you. After all, you agreed to do a day's work for a silver coin. Now, take your pay and go home. I want to give this man who was hired last as much as I have given you. Don't I have the right to do as I wish with my own money? Or are you jealous because I am generous?" Matthew 20:12-15 (From the Gospel for the Eighteenth Sunday After Pentecost)

The World

Fourteen old comic books, three one dollar bills, two signs (message given below).

This sign says: "Sell your old comic books here. Ten for one dollar." If you had a stack of comics that you didn't want anymore, you'd probably think that was a good deal. So you'd run home, take these 10 comic books, and go back to the store.

When you get back, two other kids are ahead of you. One has this stack of comics—only three. Yet the storekeeper gives him a dollar. The other has only this one, but he also receives a dollar. You think, "Wow, if they got a buck for only a few, I'll get four or five dollars for mine."

But the storekeeper also gives you a dollar. You might tell him that it's not fair for you to get a dollar for 10 comic books while someone else got a dollar for 1. But He could point to his sign and tell you he had kept his part of the deal. He gave you what he said he would. He also has the right to give his money to someone else if he wants to.

Jesus told a story like this about workers in a field. Our Savior is not telling us how to manage our money. But He is showing us what it means that we are saved by God's grace and not by our works.

God also has a sign. It says, "I gave you My Son to pay for all your sins." We can come to Christ, who has died in our place, and receive a new life with Him.

Those of us who have known Jesus as our Savior all of our lives sometimes forget that God has made the deal that gives us life with Him. When we go to church, study the Bible, help other people, we sometimes start to think that we are earning our place with God.

Then we hear that God accepts other people who have not always served Him. Some people start believing in Him only a short time before they die, yet they go to heaven just like we do. Others do not serve Him as faithfully as we do, yet they receive the same blessing from God.

Is that fair? Yes, if we believe we are saved by God's grace in Jesus Christ. It is only unfair if we think we are earning our salvation. We still have reasons to work for God and to serve Him, even though He has already saved us. We serve Him because He loves us and we love Him. Our work for God does not earn anything. But working for God now is a joy, because it shows we can be with Him even while we live on earth.

Jesus Wants to Trade with You

The Word

Jesus said, "For John the Baptist came to you showing you the right path to take, and you would not believe him; but the tax collectors and the prostitutes believed him. Even when you saw this, you did not change your minds later on and believe him." Matthew 21:32 (From the Gospel for the Nineteenth Sunday After Pentecost)

The World

Three plastic bags—one with a small piece of candy in it (a), another with two unwrapped candy cars (b), and the third with five empty candy boxes or wrappers (c). (If this Sunday is near Halloween, the message may be adapted to a trick or treat situation.)

If I had this sack of candy (b) and you had this one (a), would you trade? Sure you would. You can see the one little piece of candy in your bag. But look at the candy in mine. You'd do better if you traded.

But if I had this one (a) and you had this one (c), would you swap? You probably wouldn't, because you can see that I have two candy bars. But you have lots of candy in yours. If I tried to talk you into trading, you might think I was trying to cheat you.

Now I must show you something. See—all the wrappers and boxes in this sack (c) are empty. You should have traded, because the candy in this sack (b) is real.

Let's use the three sacks of candy to learn something about our Bible reading. Jesus was speaking to the religious leaders of His day, the kind of people that everyone said were good. He said, "For John the Baptist came to you showing you the right path to take, and you would not believe him; but the tax collectors and the prostitutes believed him. Even when you saw this, you did not change your minds later on and believe him."

Jesus is like this sack (b) of candy. He came to offer to trade His life for the lives of people. Those who knew they were bad because everyone said they were bad were like this sack (a). They were glad to trade lives with Jesus. They were glad to have His goodness and to give Him their sins.

But those who thought they were good because everyone said they were good were like this sack (c). They didn't want to trade with Jesus because they thought they were better than He. They didn't know that all the good things they did only looked good to other people. In God's eyes their good deeds were empty like the candy boxes.

Jesus speaks these words to warn us. He also wants to trade His life for your life. He wants you to know you need Him. Don't depend upon yourself. He has given His life for you. And He wants your life now.

What Holds Your Life Together?

The Word

Jesus said to them, "Haven't you ever read what the Scriptures say? 'The very stone which the builders rejected turned out to be the most important stone. This was done by the Lord; how wonderful it is!'" Matthew 21:42 (From the Gospel for the Twentieth Sunday After Pentecost)

The World

A box tied shut with string and containing large beads.

Suppose you received this (the box) for a gift. It's fun to open a gift, so you would untie the string, throw it away, and look inside. See, the box is filled with beads. But look—the beads are not on a string. You have to string them yourself. Here are the instructions. It tells you to use the string that had been tied around the box. But remember—you threw it away. So you have to go find the string and hope that it has not been taken out to the garbage.

When you find the string (retrieve it), you could string the beads and use the gift. (Start stringing beads.)

In our Bible reading today Jesus quotes Psalm 118 from the Old Testament to say that some people treated Him like I did the string in the story I just told you. He says the builders were making a stone building. They threw out one large stone because they thought it wouldn't fit in the building they planned. But later it became the cornerstone—the most important part of the building.

And Jesus said that many people treated Him the same way. Some did not like what Jesus said and did when He was on earth. They finally threw Him out. They had Him arrested and killed. But three days later He came back from the dead. He became the most important person on earth. He offers His life as a new life to all people. He holds us all together.

Each of us should listen to this warning from Jesus. We might also try to throw Him out of our lives. We get so busy. We want to do so many things. We need our education, job, family, house, car, vacation, clothes, and other things. These things often become like beads without a string. We want them, but after we get them, we find they do not make us as happy as we thought they would.

When we plan our lives to include many things but not Jesus, we have nothing to hold our lives together. Some of the things make us happy for a while. But nothing on earth will last forever. We can enjoy the many good things that can be a part of our lives here. But we need something to hold the other things together.

And that something is Jesus. Look at Jesus as this string. Everything you plan to do in life should go on the string. (Put more beads on the string.) We can enjoy all of life here when we know we have something that holds us together not only for now but also forever.

The Invitation Is for All

The Word

Jesus said, "The kingdom of heaven is like a king who prepared a wedding feast for his son. He sent his servants to tell the invited guests to come to the feast, but they did not want to come. . . . Then he called his servants, 'My wedding feast is ready,' he said, 'but the people I invited did not deserve it. Now go to the main street and invite to the feast as many people as you find.' So the servants went out into the streets and gathered all the people they could find, good and bad alike; and the wedding hall was filled with people." Matthew 22:2-3, 8-10 (From the Gospel for Twenty-first Sunday After Pentecost)

The World

A box of used crayons, including a variety of colors and sizes.

Jesus told a story about a wedding to teach us about the kingdom of heaven. He said that many were invited to the wedding who would not come. So the host invited others until the wedding hall was filled.

Like the wedding, some will go to heaven and some will not. We wonder how the people will be divided. We could understand if God would not let anyone in heaven, since we are all sinners. Or it would be easier to understand if He let everyone in. But why some and not others is difficult for us to understand. In the story Jesus told, the host of the wedding said that those who were not there "did not deserve it." How can some people deserve heaven and others not?

We'll use this box of crayons to help answer the question. Your job is to sort the crayons. Keep some and throw away the others. You might decide to keep the long, new crayons and throw away the short, broken ones. If God sorted people that way, He would keep those who appear good and refuse those who appear bad. But Jesus says that He invites both the good and the bad. God does not decide who will be in heaven that way.

Or you could keep the colors you like and throw away those you don't. You might like red, blue, and black and throw away green, brown, and pink. But God doesn't choose that way. In His story Jesus says everyone is invited. God loves all people. Christ is the Savior of all.

When Jesus said that some did not deserve heaven, He was talking only about those who refused the invitation. All were invited. Some were too busy with other things. They preferred to have their own party rather than go to the one to which they were invited.

We can't show how some crayons refuse to be saved. But we can look at our lives. We need to know how much God loves us and wants us to be with Him. We need to know what Jesus did for us when He died on the cross to pay for our sins so we could be with Him forever. We need to know that He rose from the dead to give us eternal life.

We can't be too busy to accept an invitation to be with anyone who loves us that much.

Give to Country and/or God

The Word

So Jesus said to them, "Well, then, pay to the Emperor what belong to him, and pay to God what belongs to God." Matthew 22:21 (From the Gospel for the Twenty-second Sunday After Pentecost)

The World

Two large paper disks of different color, "God" printed on one and "Country" on the other. Smaller disks, but still large enough to be read by all, each with one of the following: Money, Time, Family, Job, Education, Fun. Tape.

When some people tried to put Jesus in a bad spot by asking if it was right to pay taxes, He answered, "Pay to the Emperor what belongs to him, and pay to God what belongs to God." That answer is still a guideline for us. It doesn't tell us exactly what to do, but it gives us a chance to think about how we live with both government and church.

Since we don't have an emperor, let's put this sign up for the first part of the answer. (Tape "Country" to the wall.) And this sign is for God. (Tape to the wall.) These other signs are for things we must give to one or the other. (Tape them beneath the others.)

Now let's see how we divide these things between God and country. First money. Jesus didn't tell us how to divide it, but the Bible says we are to pay our taxes and also give to support our faith. So we'll tear this one in two and put one part on each. (Do it.) Our time also belong to both government and to God; so let's divide it too. Because my family is a gift from God I want most of this sign to go with God, but they are also citizens so I'll put a small part on "Country."

Some people work full time for the government; so their

"Job" sign would be on "Country." But others work full time for the church, and all of us help support both those who work for government and church; so let's also divide this one. Education must also be divided since we learn about both God and country in our studies. Fun can be a part of our life with God and a part of our life as citizens; so it must also be divided.

Now we have given to our country what belongs to our country and to God what belongs to God. But we still have two signs left. Everything else is divided, but maybe we should make one more move. We must ask: Does the country belong to God? Or does God belong to the country? Are we to give our country to God or our God to the country?

Because God is the one who created our land and gave us our government, the answer has to be that we give our country to God. (Put the country sign on the other, taping it halfway down so the words can be seen.) When God gave us His Son to be our Savior, He made us a part of a Kingdom that is greater than any country. As we live in our nation, we give to our country what belongs to it. But in doing so we are also giving our country to God by serving Him through our government.

The Way to Obey

The Word

When the Pharisees heard that Jesus had silenced the Sadducees, they came together, and one of them, a teacher of the Law, tried to trap Him with a question. "Teacher," he asked, "which is the greatest commandment in the Law?" Jesus answered, "'You must love the Lord your God with all your heart, with all your soul, and with all your mind.' This is the greatest and the most important commandment. The second most important commandment is like it: 'You must love your fellowman as yourself.' The whole Law of Moses and the teachings of the prophets depend on these two commandments." Matthew 22:34-40 (From the Gospel for the Twenty-third Sunday After Pentecost)

The World

An aluminium piepan with 10 holes punched in the bottom, several pieces of tape, a piece of red paper the size of the inside of the piepan, a sack of sugar—all on a large tray.

A man who wanted to trap Jesus with a question asked, "Which is the greatest commandment of the Law?" We still ask the same question today. Each of us would like to make some laws more important than others. We either want to make the ones we think we can keep as the most important or we want to make the ones that others break the most important.

The holes in the bottom of this piepan represent God's laws. The holes make the piepan leak. See. (Pour sugar into the pan and let it run through on the tray.) Just as the holes destroy the purpose of the pan, so our sins prevent us from living as we should.

We might think we are good enough to obey one law. (Cover one hole with tape.) Maybe we don't have some temptations that others have. Then we think that the one law we obey is the most important. But even if we can keep several laws in an outward way (cover several holes), we are still sinners. The pan still leaks even when some of the holes are covered.

To plug up the holes that are left, we could move the tapes to cover them. (Do it.) Then the first holes are open again. If we overcome one sin, we often replace it with pride and become judgmental against other people.

But Jesus had an answer. First, "You must love the Lord your God with all your heart, with all your soul, and with all your mind." And second, "You must love your fellowman as yourself."

Love does not fill just one hole. Love does not make us try to obey the Law to earn something from God. When we love God and people, we want to do what the Law says. Love helps us obey the Law because we want to, not because we have to.

That kind of love comes from Jesus. His love for us that kept all the Law in our place is like this (red paper). It covers all the holes in the pan. See. Now no sugar leaks out. (Try it.)

Instead of trying to find one or two commands that you can keep, instead of accusing others of breaking the Commandment you think is important, remember that Christ kept all the Commandments for you and everyone else. Let His love help you as you live with Him and others.

Check Your Batteries

The Word

On that day the kingdom of heaven will be like ten girls who took their oil lamps and went out to meet the bridegroom. Five of them were foolish, and the other five were wise. The foolish ones took their lamps but did not take any extra oil with them, while the wise ones took containers full of oil with their lamps. Matthew 25:1-4 (From the Gospel for the Twenty-fourth Sunday After Pentecost)

The World

Two flashlights with dead batteries (or put a piece of tape over the end of good batteries to break the connection) and an extra set of good batteries.

Jesus says that the time when He comes to judge the world will be like a group of women going out to a wedding at night. Because it was dark they took oil lamps. Today we would take flashlights, like these. As the women walked through the darkness, they used their oil lamps. Then they waited for the wedding to start and used more oil. Soon their oil was gone. In our times the flashlight batteries would be dead. See, neither light works.

The group that used this flashlight had no extra batteries. They had been thinking about other things and forgot to bring extra batteries. But those who used this light remembered that batteries do wear out. So they had an extra set. They put in the new batteries (do it) and had light to go on to the party. The others had to look for a store so they could buy batteries, and they missed the wedding.

Jesus did not tell this story to teach people in the old days to carry extra oil or us to carry extra batteries. Instead, He wants to teach us how to wait for His return to judge us. The lights are our faith. By faith we can see Jesus and know He is our Savior who will come to take us to heaven.

But our faith needs a source of strength. We need to receive God's strength so we can have faith. The batteries are like God's grace. The batteries give the power to make light, and grace is God's gift to us so we can believe. The story teaches us that we always need a supply of God's grace.

You are prepared for Christ's coming not only because you believe He is your Savior now but also because you have a way to continue to receive His grace so you can always believe. When He comes, you will not have to go find out who He is, because you will know.

God gives you His grace in the message of Christ. As long as you have your Bible and use it to hear the message of Jesus, you have the batteries of grace. With that grace you can live in His light now and continue to have a source of light forever.

A Gift Certificate from God

The Word

[Jesus ended one of His parables by saying,] "For to everyone who has, even more will be given, and he will have more than enough; but the one who has nothing, even the little he has will be taken away from him." Matthew 25:29 (From the Gospel for the Twenty-fifth Sunday After Pentecost)

The World

A gift certificate from the local store (or make one). Other "gift certificates" that say, "You may forgive everyone who hurts you today" and "You may tell everyone you know that God loves them."

This is a special kind of present called a gift certificate. The certificate means that someone has already gone to (name a local store) and paid $10. Then whoever receives the certificate can go to the store and get a $10 gift without spending money.

Now I will show you another kind of gift certificate. This one says, "You may forgive everyone who hurts you today." And this one says, "You may tell everyone you know that God loves them."

Like the other certificate these two gifts are good because someone else paid for them. Jesus Christ gave His life to pay for all sins. So He has earned forgiveness for all people. Now He lets us pass the forgiveness on to others. He loves all people, and He has told us that we can share His love with others. Jesus has paid for the gift certificates, so we can give them to others.

How many of these gift certificates from Jesus do you want? I suppose all of us would like the certificate from (name the store). With it we could get a gift for ourselves. But the gift certificates from Jesus are also for us. He gives us love and forgiveness. But He offers more than we need. He gives us so much that we can give away His gifts.

But sometimes people want Jesus' love and forgiveness only for themselves. They don't want to share it. But you can't receive love without loving others. You can't receive forgiveness unless you are willing to forgive others.

Jesus told a story about people who received His gifts. Some used the gift so they gained more. The more love and forgiveness you give away, the more you have. But one person wanted to keep the gift only for himself without using it. Then Jesus said, "For to everyone who has, even more will be given, and he will have more than enough; but the one who has nothing, even the little he has will be taken from him."

Remember Jesus is not talking about money. He is talking about His gifts that include love and forgiveness. The more we use His gifts, the more we receive.

Use the gift certificates from Jesus every chance you have.

You Can Practice What You Preach

The Word

"The teachers of the Law and the Pharisees," He [Jesus] said, "are the authorized interpreters of Moses' Law. So you must obey and follow everything they tell you to do; do not, however, imitate their actions, because they do not practice what they preach." Matthew 23:2-3 (From the Gospel for the Twenty-sixth Sunday After Pentecost)

The World

A large piece of poster paper and a marker pencil.

The Bible reading for today is from Matthew 23:2-3. I think it is an important verse from the Bible. Listen carefully to see if you agree. (Read text.) Now to help you remember where you can find this message, I'll write it down. (Write "Matthew 25:2-3" on the paper and show it.)

However, if you wanted to find what you just heard in the Bible, you would have a problem. You saw me write "Matthew 25:2-3" on this paper. But when I told you where the verse was located, I said "Matthew 23:2-3." Which do you remember: what you heard, or what you saw?

And that is the problem presented in the Bible reading. Jesus said that the church leaders of that day taught God's Word but they didn't do it. He also said that we cannot use the bad things they did as an excuse for not hearing the Word of God that they taught.

One lesson for us is this: We must learn to hear the message of Christ's love and forgiveness even from people who do not always show His love and forgiveness. Sometimes a pastor, a Sunday school teacher, or a mother or father, will teach the message of Christ and will tell us that He is our Savior, but they will not always follow the message they teach. Sometimes people use others' failures to practice what they preach as an excuse for not believing the message. But remember, the message comes from Christ—not people. Christ is the One who died for us. He has saved us.

Though we remember what we see better than what we hear, we must learn to remember the Word of God that we hear even if we do not see it in the lives of those who teach it.

Another lesson for us is this: Others may judge us by what they see us do rather than what they hear us say. If we point our fingers at church leaders and say that they don't practice what they preach, we are putting ourselves in a place of leadership and will be judged in the same way.

Because you come to church, you are saying that you love Jesus and through Him you love others. But in your life you may forget to love others. When you come here, you receive the forgiveness that Jesus offers. But in other places you may not forgive others. Then you are not practicing what you preach. None of us can live the perfect life that we preach when we talk about Jesus.

But Jesus has helped us even with that problem. He forgives also that sin. There is one way that we can practice what we preach. We can admit we are wrong. (Change the 25 to 23 on the paper.) We can ask Christ to help us correct our wrong, and we can share the message that He forgives us.

The Alarm Is Set

The Word

As Jesus sat on the Mount of Olives, the disciples came to Him in private. "Tell us when all this will be," they asked, "and what will happen to show that it is the time for Your coming and the end of the age." Jesus answered, "Watch out, and do not let anyone fool you. . . . But whoever holds out to the end will be saved." Matthew 24:3-4, 13 (From the Gospel for the Twenty-seventh Sunday After Pentecost)

The World

A clockface, without numbers, drawn on a large posterboard so any side can be the top. In addition to the two hands, have a third alarm hand made of another color.

The disciples asked Jesus a question that many people still ask today. They wanted to know when the end of the world would come. Some people think the world will last for thousands of more years. Others think it will end soon. We would like to have God's answer.

Jesus told the disciples not to let anyone fool them. And He gives us the same warning. Don't let anyone fool you into thinking the world will end next week. And don't let anyone fool you into thinking the world will never end.

We could use this alarm clock to show when the world will end. See, these two hands show what time it is, and this hand shows when the alarm is set. When the alarm goes off, the world will end.

However, you notice that the clock has no numbers. We know the alarm is set, but we can't tell what time it is. You might try to guess the time by saying the alarm looks like it is pointed to 4 o'clock. But how do you know that the top of the clock is here? Maybe the clock should be like this. (Turn it to

125

one side.) Now it looks like it might be 8 o'clock. Or it could be like this—then it's 10 o'clock. Or it's 2 o'clock this way. Don't let anyone fool you. We can tell the alarm is set, but we can't tell when it's going to ring. We know the world will end, but we don't know when.

You might wonder why we need the alarm if we don't know when it is going to ring. The alarm serves an important purpose. It reminds us that the end of the world is coming. It tells us to be ready at all times.

Many people are frightened when they think about the end of the world. They are afraid of what might happen. But Jesus promises, "Whoever holds out to the end will be saved." The end of the world should not scare us. It is a promise that Christ will return to take us to be with Him. The alarm is a happy reminder for us. It helps us remember that something good will happen when Jesus comes because He is coming to take us home with Him.

Look What You Did to Me!

The Word

Jesus said, "The King will answer back, 'I tell you, indeed, whenever you did this for one of the least important of these brothers of Mine, you did it for Me!'" and, "The King will answer them back, 'I tell you, indeed, whenever you refused to help one of these least important ones, you refused to help Me.'" Matthew 25:40, 45 (From the Gospel for the Last Sunday After Pentecost)

The World

Two pictures of Jesus, each with a child's drawing of a house on the back. (The child's drawing and the picture of Jesus may be pasted together.)

Look at these pictures that were drawn by children. (Show only the child's side of the picture.) Suppose I gave this picture to one child and the other picture to another child.

The first child might say, "Thanks for the neat picture. I like it and will put it up in my room." (Place the picture where it can be seen.)

The second child might say, "I don't like that picture. It's not pretty at all." So that child would tear the picture up and throw it away. (Tear the picture in two and drop it on the floor without showing the back side.)

Now suppose Jesus comes to the two children. To the first He says, "Thank you for keeping My picture." And to the second He says, "Why did you tear up the picture of Me and throw it away?"

The children would be surprised. They would say to Jesus, "We didn't have a picture of You. We only had pictures of houses drawn by children."

"But My picture was with the picture of the houses," Jesus would say. "See, My picture is here shown in a place of honor."

(Turn the first picture around so the picture of Jesus can be seen.) "And look (pick up the torn picture), My picture has been torn in two and thrown away."

What I did to the pictures drawn by children, I also did to the pictures of Jesus, because they were on the same paper. Jesus also tells us that whatever we do to other people, we do to Him, because He is a part of us.

Jesus tied His life to our lives when He was born as a person on earth, when He died in our place, and when He rose from the dead. When we were baptized in His name, we received Him as a part of our lives.

So whatever people do to us, they are doing to Jesus. And whatever we do to others we are doing to Jesus. Jesus tells us that when we see hungry people, we should remember they are His people. He is a part of their lives. When we feed them, we are feeding Him. When we speak kindly to people, we are speaking kindly to Jesus. When we call others bad names and hurt others, we are doing that to Jesus, because He loves them.

Think about the way you treat people and hear Jesus say, "Look what you did to Me!"